Succeeding in Family History

Helpful hints and time-saving tips

D0730637

JOHN TITFORD

COUNTRYSIDE BOOKS
NEWBURY, BERKSHIRE

First published 2001
© John Titford 2001
Reprinted 2001

COUNTRYSIDE BOOKS
3 Catherine Road
Newbury, Berkshire

To view our complete range of books,
please visit us at
www.countrysidebooks.co.uk

ISBN 1 85306 691 5

Produced through MRM Associates Ltd., Reading
Printed by Woolnough Bookbinding Ltd., Irthlingborough

Contents

Introduction

This book starts at the beginning, but is not only intended for beginners. It takes family history research in England and Wales as its focus, but will have relevance, I hope, to other family historians in the English-speaking world.

My intention has been to inform, but also to amuse, since humorous aspects of family history research can so often be found lying just beneath the surface. I have been able to draw upon material which I have gleaned over the years both as a researcher into all lines of my own family and as a professional genealogist working for others. I have also revisited some of the material sent to *Family Tree Magazine* during the time in the early 1990s when I took over responsibility for its 'Genealogical Miscellany' feature from Michael Armstrong, but also in later years after Tom Wood had taken over the 'Miscellany' and presented it in his own inimitable fashion.

It has been largely to *Family Tree Magazine* (*FTM*) readers that I have turned, then, when I have needed concrete examples of the bizarre, the humorous and the downright odd to illustrate the points I have wished to make. It would otherwise have taken a lifetime of work, and a great deal of luck, to have unearthed such material – and the same goes for some charming examples of census oddities I have quoted from Susan Lumas's book, *Making use of the census* (1992).

I make no excuse for starting with a section on names, which I hope will have relevance to readers researching families within Britain and beyond. Unless we can learn to be flexible and imaginative about the way in which surnames are spelt, and to be constantly on the lookout for naming systems and patterns, we can hardly get started on a meaningful journey through the exciting highways and byways of family history. My intention here has been to warn the beginner and to remind the experienced family historian about the crucial role that names have to play in almost everything we do.

We continue by way of Civil Registration and then Census records in

England and Wales. What I have written here is specific to these topics, but there will be much which has a broader relevance to family history as a whole. In due course, I hope to write a further volume covering other aspects of genealogical research.

If you are new to family history, be warned that it can become an all-consuming passion – not because it is a narrow topic of study, but because it is so wide and all-encompassing. Let Colin Rogers (*The Family Tree Detective*, 3rd edition, 1997) issue the warning for us officially:

> *Once you have the bug, you have it for life, and it is a bug which thrives on frustration.*

Collectors of wise words such as these are recommended to leaf through the pages of *The sunny side of genealogy* by F. D. Baselt (Genealogical Publishing Company, Baltimore, 1988) which includes gems such as the following:

> *If you think you have all the answers, maybe you haven't asked the right questions.*
> *A hobby is hard work you wouldn't do for a living.*

If I may I'll just add a couple of aphorisms of my own to set you on your way:

> *Always doubt before you believe.*
> *The more cherished an assumption is, the harder you should work to disprove it.*
> *Think laterally and flexibly.*
> *Revisit your old notes of yesterday: they may contain the answers to the questions you are asking today.*

John Titford

Acknowledgements

Family history research thrives on help and encouragement freely offered and on information generously shared. Not only that, but many family historians soon find that 'what goes around comes around': you offer help to a total stranger one day, only to find that the very next day somebody equally unknown to you is kind enough to send you an unexpected piece of vital information which aids your own research.

I am very pleased to acknowledge the help offered to me over a number of years by family, friends, colleagues and clients. In particular, I should like to express my gratitude to all those correspondents whose letters to the 'Miscellany' feature of *Family Tree Magazine* over the years have provided some wonderful examples of genealogical treasures and oddities which I have used in this book. The name of each correspondent is mentioned at the appropriate stage in the text.

I should also like to offer a special word of thanks to Susan Lumas and Mark Herber, trusty friends, who have been kind but firm in their suggestions for amendments and improvements to the text, and above all to my wife Heather, who can be relied upon to offer me honest criticism tempered by unfailing moral support.

Illustrations
I am grateful to the following for providing me with illustrative material and/or permission to reproduce copyright material:
Intellectual Reserve, inc.; Christine Selby of Leigh-on-Sea, Essex; The Building of Bath Museum; the *Daily Telegraph*; the Office for National Statistics; the Controller of Her Majesty's Stationery Office; the Public Record Office. Some material in this publication is reprinted by permission of The Church of Jesus Christ of Latter-day Saints. In granting permission for the use of copyrighted material, the Church does not imply endorsement or authorization of this publication.

CHAPTER 1

Names

Without names there would be no family history. We would know that we were descended from a great number of ancestors, but would have no means of identifying them in any meaningful way. We'd still be at the starting gate.

For all that, few enough personal names are unique identifiers, especially in earlier centuries when the available pool of first names was more limited than it is today and children were not named after singers or after film or soap opera stars.

In February 1994 Mrs J. Kembo from Gillingham in Kent reported to *Family Tree Magazine* that she had been reading a book called *Norfolk remembered* by Robert Bagshaw, which revealed the fact that at one time there were no fewer than 16 men in Beeston Road, Sheringham, called John Henry Grice. What a nightmare! It appears that various Sheringham fishing families guarded their women folk jealously from the attention of outsiders, and inter-married within a close family network.

Spare a thought, too, for Glyn Jones of Newark, who had been doing his best to unravel his Jones ancestry in Wales. Searching the 1851 census seemed like a good idea, even if Glyn was looking for a 'John Jones'. Alas, there were no fewer than 47 John Joneses, father and son, in the parish of Eglwysfach, Caernarvon. No problem – Glyn knew the name of the family farm, Maes-y-Groes. Oh, no – there were two farms of that name in the parish, Upper and Lower, but with this helpful distinction often omitted. Never mind, there were servants. Sorry, the servants at both farms had the same names ... (*FTM*, May 1994).

So few names are unique – even when a person carries two forenames and one surname, as the Grices did in the example quoted – but at least the fact that surnames are inherited offers us a sporting chance of making some progress and of generating a meaningful pedigree. From names we can move to pedigrees, and from pedigrees to the wider perspective of a family's history in time and place. But names are the starting point.

Surnames

Successful family history research in most countries in the Western World depends above all on the existence of hereditary surnames. Many unimpeachable Welsh pedigrees of early date proceed by way of first names only, and the Maoris of New Zealand and others can make a breathtaking oral recitation of much of their ancestry by heart, but for most European and American researchers it is the fact that surnames have been passed down from one generation to the next in the male line that makes it possible for us to peel away the generations and to construct pedigrees which have at least a more-than-even chance of being reliable. The custom of using surnames developed around the 12th and 13th centuries in England, before which time our forebears would have carried only one personal name; eventually these 'added' or 'extra' names became hereditary, a custom which began with the nobility and gradually spread to the common man in town and country during the next two centuries.

Surnames are our guide, then, but they can so easily lead us astray along many a rocky road or down many a cul-de-sac. It is never too early to learn to treat surnames both with respect and also with some degree of caution.

**Expect to find distinctive surname systems operating in different countries

We must beware of assuming that naming patterns are the same the world over. Some practices common in the islands of the Pacific would throw most Western family historians into a flat spin. In the Cook Islands, for example, the father's first name is taken as the surname of the next generation – a fact further complicated by the fact that in the Cooks, and in Hawaii, a male was allowed to have three wives concurrently and that Hawaiians married half-brothers and sisters to keep the line pure (Lois Moreland, *FTM*, June 1994).

An American friend of mine from San Francisco, Harvey Good, studied for his medical degree at Puebla in Mexico. When I wrote letters to him at that stage in his life, I would address them to 'Harvey Good Rosales', to conform to the Spanish-speaking pattern. 'Good' was his American father's surname, while 'Rosales' was his Nicaraguan-born mother's maiden name, and had to be placed last in the sequence.

Most Welsh surnames are patronymic in origin, and many in centuries

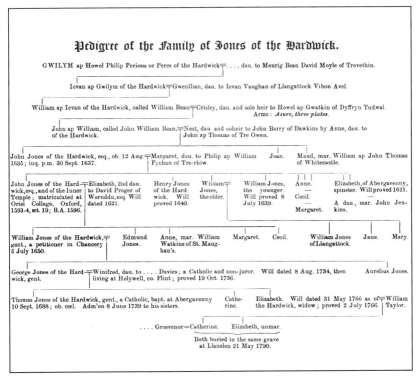

Pedigree of the Family of Jones of the Hardwick.

GWILYM ap Howel Philip Perious or Peres of the Hardwick⊤.... dau. to Meurig Bean David Moyle of Trevethin.

Ievan ap Gwilym of the Hardwick⊤Gwenllian, dau. to Ievan Vaughan of Llangattock Vibon Avel.

William ap Ievan of the Hardwick, called William Bean⊤Crisley, dau. and sole heir to Howel ap Gwatkin of Dyffryn Tudwal. Arms: *Azure, three plates.*

John ap William, called John William Bean,⊤Nest, dau. and coheir to John Barry of Dawkins by Anne, dau. to of the Hardwick. John ap Thomas of Tre Owen.

John Jones of the Hardwick, esq., ob. 12 Aug.⊤Margaret, dau. to Philip ap William Joan. Maud, mar. William ap John Thomas 1635; inq. p.m. 30 Sept. 1637. Fychan of Tre-rhiw. of Whitecastle.

John Jones of the Hard-⊤Elizabeth, 2nd dau. Henry Jones William⊤ William Jones, Anne. Elizabeth, of Abergavenny, wick,esq.,and of the Inner to David Proger of of the Hard- Jones, the younger. — spinster. Will proved 1621. Temple; matriculated at Wernddu,esq. Will wick. Will the elder. Will proved 8 Cecil. Oriel College, Oxford, dated 1621. proved 1640. July 1639. — A dau., mar. John Jen- 1593-4, æt. 19; B.A. 1596. Margaret. kins.

William Jones of the Hardwick,⊤ Edmund Anne, mar. William Margaret. Cecil. William Jones Jane. Mary. gent., a petitioner in Chancery Jones. Watkins of St. Maug- of Llangattock. 5 July 1650. han's.

George Jones of the Hard-⊤Winifred, dau. to .... Davies; a Catholic and non-juror. Will dated 8 Aug. 1734, then Aurelius Jones. wick, gent. living at Holywell, co. Flint; proved 19 Oct. 1736.

Thomas Jones of the Hardwick, gent., a Catholic, bapt. at Abergavenny Cathe- Elizabeth. Will dated 31 May 1766 as of⊤William 10 Sept. 1688; ob. cœl. Adm'on 8 June 1739 to his sisters. rine. the Hardwick, widow; proved 2 July 1766. Taylor.

.... Grosvenor=Catherine. Elizabeth, unmar.

Both buried in the same grave at Llanelen 21 May 1790.

Keeping up with the Joneses. *The pedigree of Jones of the Hardwick begins with a patronymic naming pattern: Ievan son of Gwilym is 'Ievan ap Gwilym', his son William is 'William ap Ievan' and William's son John is 'John ap William'. John's Christian name then becomes a hereditary surname, passed down to succeeding generations, beginning with his eldest son 'John Jones' (John, son of John). Thus the family of 'Jones' has been born. (From Sir Joseph Alfred Bradney's* History of Monmouthshire, *1906)*

past were not hereditary surnames at all. Hugh, son of William, would be called 'Hugh Williams'; his son David would be called 'David Hughes', while David's son Evan would be called 'Evan Davies' – and so on. This has often made the tracing of Welsh pedigrees a difficult if not impossible task! The Welsh prefix 'ap' (or 'ab' before a vowel) means 'son of'. This might be shortened as time went by, so that Hugh the son of Richard, originally 'Hugh ap Richard', might eventually become 'Hugh Pritchard'. Surnames with this origin include Probert, Pumphrey, Pugh, Powell (ap Howell), Pryce (ap Rhys), Bowen and Bevan.

Even as late as 1853, the Registrar General had this to say in his *Sixteenth Report*:

> *In Wales, however, the* surnames, *if surnames they can be called, do not present the same variety, most of them having been formed in a simple manner from the Christian or fore- name of the father in the genitive case,* son *being understood. Thus, Evan's son became* **Evans,** *John's son* **Jones,** *&c. Others were derived from the father's name coalesced with a form of the word* ap *or* hab *(son of), by which Hugh ap Howell became* **Powell,** *Evan ap Hugh became* **Pugh,** *and in like manner were formed nearly all the Welsh surnames beginning with the letters B and P. Hereditary surnames were not in use even amongst the gentry of Wales until the time of Henry VIII, nor were they generally established until a much later period; indeed, at the present day they can scarcely be said to be adopted amongst the lower classes in the wilder districts, where, as the marriage registers show, the Christian name of the father still frequently becomes the patronymic of the son in the manner just described.*

**Be open-minded and flexible in your consideration of surnames

It is often said that the greatest single difference between professional and amateur family historians is that the professional takes a more flexible approach to the form and spelling of a surname. Indeed, the professional can afford to do just that, since he or she will lack the emotional attachment to the spelling of a name which may blind us if we are studying our family. As an amateur, do try to stand back and be detached; refuse to be protective or precious about your surname in its present-day 'correct' spelling, and be aware that many surnames have adopted different forms in various places and at various times.

Local dialect, accent or intonation, speech impediments, the inability of parish clerks and others to spell consistently – all have taken their toll on surname spelling, especially at a time when most people were illiterate. In Britain, it was only the advent of compulsory education in the 19th century that began to effect some kind of stability, establishing surnames in the way that we spell them today.

It may prove to be significant that your branch of the family spells its name Fyson with a 'y', while others are Fison with an 'i', but in times past it is just as likely that your original ancestors would have used either version indiscriminately.

Sometimes it is consonants in names which vary – Fosse may be the same as Vosse, Fenn the same as Venn – and you should always be on the look-out for dropped or added 'h's, whereby Halfords become

Alfords and Alfords become Halfords. Generally, however, it is vowels which lead to the greatest instability in names, since you do not use your tongue, your lips or your teeth to affect the sound as it comes up from your voice-box, and the merest difference in the shape of your mouth as you speak can move you from one vowel to another. Historically, the Wiltshire surname Titford began life as Totford, then became Tutford, flirted with the variety Tetford for a while, then settled down as Titford, but with a Hampshire variety of Tatford. In other words, it has used the entire gamut of vowels, a, e, i, o and u at various times. You don't have to take a family historian's word for this: it is clear from the Wiltshire volume of the publications of the English Place-Name Society (1939) that the village of North Tidworth (known locally as 'Tedworth') was originally Todeworth and then Tuddewurth. Here, based upon written evidence, we have a Wiltshire place-name following the same vowel development as the Wiltshire surname of Totford/Tutford/Titford. Clearly a consistent pattern was at work here, evident also in the Wiltshire place-names Dinton, Stitchcombe, Tidpit and others.

Even in recent times I have had correspondence addressed to me using a bewildering range of surname spelling variations, some the result of a typing error, others caused by mis-hearing, mis-reading or mis-copying.

I've had contact with family historians who have had to live with the fact that the surname Cottington can also be Cottingham; that Chamin can be Chamond; that Sainty can be Sankey; that Mauger can be Major or Mayer; that Gunny can be Gunning; that Harwood can be Huddard, Hurred, Harrod – or even Herring; that Smurthwaite can be Smirfit, Smurfeit or Smorfit; that Lawton can be Layton; that Levick can be Leathwick, Leavick, Loavick, Levicke or Levycke; that Clute can be Clout, Clowt (or even Clot ...); that Gaught can be Gout, Gault or Golt and that Towell can be Towelle, Towells, Towelles, Touell, Toule, Toulle, Touelle, Towyll, Towl, Towle or Townhill. The surname Clive, hastily written, can readily be mis-read as Olive – and so on. Most surname dictionaries will cross-reference entries which are known to belong together, and the International Genealogical Index (IGI) has its own (occasionally eccentric) method of grouping known variations together. Boyd's Marriage Index, which you can consult at the Society of Genealogists and elsewhere, can be even more eccentric on occasions; if you can't find entries for the surname Phillips, for example, it's worth looking under the bizarre variant of Filips and the like.

I once worked for an American client who only wanted references to emigrants from England whose surname 'Cook' was spelt with an 'e' at the end. I carried out the work with a heavy heart, warning him as I did so that his chances of success in locating a particular ancestor were severely reduced by this unfortunate fixation.

358	LINCOLN CONSISTORY COURT

Vavasour, Vavisor, Matthew, Ropsley, 1614 : I, 312
,,   William, Ropsley, 1612 : Axi, 26
,,   Vavister, Alice, sister of William Vavister, and legatee in the will
        of Matthew, Ropsley, 1612 : T, Axi, 29

A surname on the move before our very eyes. *A calendar of Letters of Administration featuring a connected set of individuals in Ropsley, Lincolnshire, includes Matthew* Vavisor, *William* Vavasour *and Alice* Vavister, *sister of William* Vavister. *Different branches of the family subsequently adopted the variants* Bavister *and* Vawser. *(From* Calendars of administrations in the Consistory Court of Lincoln 1540–1659. *Index Library, vol.52, 1921)*

I have a friend who hails originally from Whittlesey in Cambridgeshire called Steve Bavister; his surname had always struck me as being unusual, and I used to collect references to it and send them to Steve whenever I could. Many years later I found myself doing some research for a Miss Vawser of March in Cambridgeshire; imagine my surprise when I found out that the surnames Bavister and Vawser were in effect one and the same! The common origin was the Yorkshire surname Vavasour.

P.H. Reaney's *Dictionary of British surnames* (1995) had already alerted me to the fact that Vawser was 'a syncopated form of Vavasour', and I needed a link from March, in the Isle of Ely in Cambridgeshire, back to Yorkshire. Sure enough, the 1662 will of William Vawser of March, the first member of the family to live there, mentions his land in Bawtry in Yorkshire. He had presumably moved south to snap up some cheap fertile land once the Fens had been drained.

Another branch of the Vavasour family chose to settle in Emneth in Cambridgeshire, and a baptism entry in the parish register there for 11th January 1816 reads: 'Sarah, daughter of Thomas and Ann Bavister, alias Vavazor, of Emneth, farmer'.

As if it weren't difficult enough to keep track of surnames that have changed according to time and place, there are those which, like some place-names, seem to have been pronounced in a way that bears little enough resemblance to their spelling. This is particularly true of certain surnames borne by the wealthier classes: Grosvenor is pronounced 'Grovenor'; Fiennes is 'Fines'; Waldegrave is 'Waldgrave'; Beauchamp is 'Beecham' and Villiers is 'Villers'. The longest single English surname, Featherstonehaugh, can be 'Fanshaw'. Some Scottish names are no more helpful than this: Dalziel is pronounced 'Deeyell', Menzies is often pronounced 'Mingis', and Marjoribanks is 'Marchbanks'.

Mark Twain must have noticed this frustrating propensity of some British names to confound all reasonable expectations, and exaggerated it to witty effect: 'The common Welsh name *Bzjxxllwcp*,' he wrote, 'is pronounced *Jackson*.'

Let nothing surprise you, then – be flexible and imaginative, since almost anything is possible! Do take this approach to surnames to heart very early on in your research; it will take more time as you wade through indexes to check for all the variations you can think of, but even that is preferable to having to return later and to start looking for new variants all over again.

**Treat Surname Dictionaries with a degree of caution

Surname dictionaries – those by C.W. Bardsley, P.H. Reaney, H. Harrison, C.L'E. Ewen and P. Hanks and F. Hodges being the best-known – can be exceptionally useful when it comes to determining the meaning and origin of names, but beware relying on them too heavily. They cover a wide field, and are bound to be speculative or inaccurate in places. If yours is an unusual surname, it's quite likely that as time goes by it will be you, not the authors of well-known books, who will become the world expert on its origin and distribution.

The only truly reliable guide to the origin of any particular surname, and the variations that it has undergone according to time and place, is the existence of solid evidence taken from written sources, whatever so-called experts in the linguistic aspects of name-change may have to say. This is why a book by George Redmonds entitled *Surnames and genealogy: a new approach* (New England Historic Genealogical Society, Boston, USA, 1997) makes such refreshing reading: George records what actually happened to a number of surnames in practice, not what might have happened in theory.

One book cast in a different mould but which has surnames as its focus is still very useful: *Homes of family names in Great Britain* by H.B. Guppy (1890) makes little attempt to define the origin and meaning of names, but it does give scores of examples of surnames in use, county by county, and carries an alphabetical list of English and Welsh surnames, giving the frequency of each in contemporary directories, thus allowing you to see where particular names were most frequently found at the period. Neither modern telephone directories nor information available on the Internet or on CD-ROMs have rendered Guppy's book entirely redundant.

Buttery. Nottinghamshire, 12; Yorkshire, North and East Ridings, 9.

Button. Suffolk, 26.

Buxton. Cheshire, 9; Derbyshire, 43; Staffordshire, 26.

Byard. Derbyshire, 13.

Byford. Essex, 21.

Byrd. Worcestershire, 18.

Byron. Nottinghamshire, 16.

Cade. Lincolnshire, 7.

Cadle. Gloucestershire, 14.

Cadwallader. Shropshire, 17.

Cæsar. Surrey, 20.

Caines. Dorsetshire, 15. (*See* Cane.)

Cairns. Northumberland, 18.

Cake. Dorsetshire, 15.

Calcutt. Oxfordshire, 18. Caldecott—Coldicott. Cheshire, 9; Gloucestershire, 17; Shropshire, 10; Worcestershire, 22. In Gloucestershire, Coldicott is more generally found. In Worcestershire, the two names are equally represented. Calcutt in Oxfordshire is an evident contraction.

Caldwell. Lancashire, 8. (*See* Cauldwell.)

Callender. Durham, 24.

Callow. Herefordshire, 14.

Callwood. Cheshire, 9.

Calver. Suffolk, 16.

Calvert. Yorkshire, West Riding, 18; Yorkshire, North and East Ridings, 24.

Camm. Gloucestershire, 17; Nottinghamshire, 12.

Cammack. Lincolnshire, 7.

Camp. Derbyshire, 13; Hertfordshire, 22.

Campion. Lincolnshire, 11; Northamptonshire, 15.

Campkin. Hertfordshire, 18.

Candy. Hampshire, 21; Somersetshire, 29; Wiltshire, 13.

Cane—Caine. Hampshire, 17; Sussex, 18. (*See* Caines.)

Cann. Cornwall, 9; Devonshire, 13; Norfolk, 9.

Cannell. Norfolk, 17.

Canning. Hampshire, 21; Warwickshire, 24; Wiltshire, 9.

Cannon. Hertfordshire, 54; Somersetshire, 9.

Cant. Essex, 15.

Cantrell — Cantrill. Staffordshire, 10.

Capes. Lincolnshire, 7.

Capon. Kent, 9; Suffolk, 42.

Capstick. Yorkshire, West Riding, 15.

Cardell. Cornwall, 20.

Cardwell. Lancashire, 8.

Careless. Worcestershire, 22.

Carey—Cary. Somersetshire, 24.

Carlyon. Cornwall, 12.

Carmichael. Northumberland, 41.

Carne. Cornwall, 8.

Carpenter. Cornwall, 9; Devonshire, 7; Oxfordshire, 30; Somersetshire, 27; Suffolk, 11; Wiltshire, 30.

Carr. Cheshire, 12; Cumberland and Westmoreland, 35; Durham, 16; Lancashire, 16; Leicestershire and Rutlandshire, 17 Northumberland, 50; Sussex, 21; York-

The frequency of surnames. *In his book* Homes of family names in Great Britain *(1890), H.B. Guppy gives a number against each surname to represent the frequency of its occurrence in various counties according to the samples he had collected.*

**Pay special attention to surname aliases

It can be confusing to come across references in written or printed documents to 'Ralph Smith, alias Jones' or 'als Jones' or 'otherwise Jones'. Which was the 'proper' surname? How did the two become yoked together in this way, and for what purpose?

There may be one of several reasons:

● If a mother remarried, her children might take the surname of their new step-father, with their original surname as an alias – or vice-versa.

● A person might adopt an alias according to the terms of a will in which he or she is a beneficiary, though in such cases a complete change of surname is a more usual practice.

● Illegitimacy often gave rise to the use of two alternative surnames; a child might bear the maiden surname of the mother and also that of the father, one acting as an alias.

● When a couple were living together but were not married, the common-law wife may be entered in records under her maiden name, with the surname of her partner as an alias. Any children born to the couple might bear this same double surname.

● Some tenants who held copyhold land in more than one manor could be known by a different form of an alias in each, being referred to as 'James Batt, alias Boxall' in one manor, and 'James Boxall, alias Batt' in the other.

● Sometimes the term 'alias' is used when there are two or more possible spellings of the surname, each accepted by the individual in question: 'Matthew Cook alias Coke'.

Aliases are uncommon at the present day, many having been abandoned or converted into a 'double-barrelled' surname such as 'Smith-Jones', though members of the community who find it useful to confound the authorities by having more than one identity may be referred to as 'James Wilkinson *aka* ['also known as'] Roberts'.

**Consider the possibility that what appears to be an inherited surname may have been a name given to a foundling

Foundlings have long been a sad but almost inevitable feature of human life, ever since Pharaoh's daughter found Moses in the bull-rushes. Those abandoned children who were found and saved from starvation were the lucky ones, but they posed a problem to the parish authorities

in centuries past. What should the anonymous child be called? A glance
at parish registers or at churchwardens' or overseers' accounts makes it
clear that the usual ploy was to call the unfortunate after the town, the
parish or the street in which he or she had been found. As a result, a last
name which might give the appearance of having always been an
inherited surname, may have started life as nothing of the kind:

> *A child out of Seething Lane, named Charles Parish.*
> *Christened.*
> *A child found in Mark Lane, and christd. Mark Lane.* (Both
> from the registers of All Hallows Barking, London, no date
> given)
> *Job Rakt-out-of the Asshes, being borne the last of August in*
> *the lane going to Sir John Spencer's back gate, and there laide*
> *in a heape of seacole asshes, was baptized the first daye of*
> *September following, and dyed the next day after.* (St Helen's
> Bishopsgate, London, 1612)
> *Mary Porch, a foundling, baptised 18 Jan. 1618.* (St Dunstan
> in the West, London)

My own favourite in this category comes from an entry I once
stumbled across in the original parish register for St Pancras, London:

> *William Euston. Child found in a box in a railway carriage at*
> *Euston Station. Baptised 14th July, 1894.*

I had always thought that there was a real flavour of Lady Bracknell
in Oscar Wilde's play *The Importance of Being Earnest* here, as she
responds with incredulity to being told by an apparently respectable
young man that he had been found as a baby in a handbag on the
railway (the Brighton line): 'A handbag! ... The line is immaterial!' It
was only when Raymond Ryden kindly wrote to me from Farnborough
in Hampshire in November 1999, however, that I realised that the
connexion I had made with Wilde had more relevance to it than I had
ever imagined. Raymond had recently attended a performance of
Earnest in Chichester, and found the following information in the
programme, beginning with a cutting from a Worthing newspaper of
1894:

> *A BABY IN A HAMPER. On Monday a man took a hamper*
> *to the goods department of the Great Northern Railway,*
> *King's Cross, and requested that it should be forwarded to a*
> *lady at Richmond. A short time afterwards one of the officials*
> *put the hamper on the weighing machine in order to obtain the*

In a handbag?! *A child was found in a box in a railway carriage at Euston Station in July 1894, and was christened at nearby St Pancras church under the name of 'William Euston'. Reading about this unfortunate foundling in a Worthing newspaper gave Oscar Wilde one of the key ideas he was to use in his play,* The Importance of Being Earnest. *(Euston Station, from Walford's* Old and New London)

weight before dispatching it, when he heard a noise. The hamper was immediately opened, and a baby about a fortnight old was discovered wrapped in wadding, with a feeding bottle by its side. A constable was sent for, and the child was taken to the police-station. No trace of the man who left the hamper has been found. (Worthing Gazette, *11 June 1894)*

It was in the summer of 1894, while on holiday with his family in the town of Worthing, that Wilde wrote The Importance of Being Earnest. *Many of its lines have become part of modern British folklore and it appears that Jack Worthing's humble origins, as the baby abandoned in a handbag in the cloakroom of Victoria Station's Brighton line, probably owe their existence to the local Worthing newspaper. The* Worthing Gazette *was running a story entitled 'A baby in a hamper' during Wilde's stay in the town.*

The author of this piece might have added that we now know how it was that the play's character Jack Worthing acquired his name. So it very much looks here as if the parish register entry I had come across by pure chance had a direct relevance to Wilde after all. The timing is right – the discovery of the child was reported in the Worthing newspaper in June 1894, and William Euston was baptised the following month. King's Cross Station is within the parish of St Pancras, where the baptism took place, and the only inconsistency we are left with is that the parish register claims that the child was found at Euston Station, while the newspaper account speaks of King's Cross, just along the road, which was home to the Great Northern Railway Company. The object lesson here, I guess, is to be sure to copy down interesting or unusual material you come across in your research into a book or a file named 'Miscellaneous' or some such. You never know when it might come in useful!

**Consider the possibility that a surname might have been changed during a person's lifetime

If you can't find evidence of an ancestor's birth or baptism, it is perhaps too easy to assume that the person concerned must have changed his or her surname during their lifetime. Don't come to this conclusion too readily – but do be aware that many people did change their name for various reasons:

To avoid mockery

A surname like Kennedy is a safe enough one to bear, since most people are unaware that its meaning, from the Celtic, is 'Ugly head'. Similarly, the Norfolk branch of the family of Sherborn (alias Sherborne, Sherbourn, Sherbourne, Sherbon, Sherburn, Shereburne, Sheerburne, Shearburn, Sharborne, Shirburn, Shirborn, Shirburne, Shireborne, Shirebourne, Shireburne, Shurborne, Scireburn, Scyreburne, Schyrebourne, Shyreburne, Schirburn, Schireburne, Schyreburne, Scyrburne, Cherbron, Churborne, etc) was originally known as Sharnborn, meaning 'dung stream'. Earlier bearers of such a name might have been tempted to change it, given its unfortunate connotations, though in modern times the 'dung' origin is long lost and Sharnborn would cause no more of a stir than the Bedfordshire place-name Sharnbrook ('dung brook') – which is more than can be said for its Bedfordshire neighbour Shillington, which was spelt Shitlington until the late 18th century (meaning 'Hill of Scyttel's people' – no reference to dung), when it assumed its present less shocking form.

Things would have been rather different, however, for a lady by the

  ☐ **1.** Abigail GOTOBED - International Genealogical Index
Gender: F Marriage: 2 Feb 1704 Of, Over, Cambridge, England

  ☐ **2.** Abigail GOTOBED - International Genealogical Index
Gender: F Marriage: 2 Feb 1704 Of Over, Cambridge, England

  ☐ **3.** Abigail GOTOBED - International Genealogical Index
Gender: F Marriage: 2 Feb 1704 Over, Cambridge, England

  ☐ **4.** Ada Eleanor Gee GOTOBED - International Genealogical Index
Gender: F Christening: 1 Feb 1869 Old Church, Saint Pancras, London, England

  ☐ **5.** Agnes GOTTOBED - International Genealogical Index
Gender: F Christening: 17 Feb 1599 Chesterton, Cambridge, England

  ☐ **6.** Agnes GOETOBED - International Genealogical Index
Gender: F Christening: 15 Sep 1616 Southill, Bedford, England

  ☐ **7.** Albert John GOTOBED - International Genealogical Index
Gender: M Christening: 6 Sep 1874 All Saints And Saint John, Hertford, Hertford, England

  ☐ **8.** Alfred GOTOBED - International Genealogical Index
Gender: M Christening: 16 Oct 1832 Saint Mary-Wesleyan, Ely, Cambridge, England

  ☐ **9.** Alfred GOTOBED - International Genealogical Index
Gender: M Christening: 14 Feb 1836 Saint Mary-Wesleyan, Ely, Cambridge, England

Gone to bed, *The surname of 'Gotobed' was once fairly common in Cambridgeshire and elsewhere, but has become scarcer over the years as many members of the family have decided to adopt euphemistic alternatives. (From the on-line version of the Church of Jesus Christ of Latter-day Saints'* International Genealogical Index, *at: www.familysearch.org)* [Reprinted by permission. Copyright © 1980, 1999, by Intellectual Reserve, Inc.]

name of Agnes Sylicowe, who married Thomas Hall at the London church of St Nicholas Acons in 1570; how tempted she must have been to change that name, before Mr Hall did it for her at the altar! Those bearing the surname Death have long favoured the spelling D'Eath – which, as it happens, more faithfully reflects what may have been its French origin – and if a person named Sidebottom doesn't actually change the spelling to Sidebotham, he or she still might insist on the pronunciation 'Siddybotohm'.

R.J. Pearson of Fairy Meadow, New South Wales, wrote to *Family Tree Magazine* in August 1994, telling us that his mother's maiden name was Harse – rare enough in Australia, but not so rare in Somerset, the home of his mother's family until they emigrated in the 1850s. 'Some members of the family have deliberately changed the spelling, one reason being that so many people do not sound their "aitches"! One member of the family was very particular in emphasising that his name was "Hurse" and not "Harse". When he became engaged to be married to a Miss Head, his friends dubbed them "Tops and tails", but when he returned from his honeymoon and was greeted by one of them exclaiming "Here comes 'arse over 'ead" it was just too much, and thereafter his name was definitely "Hurse"!'

Some courageous people have chosen to stick with surnames like Daft, Bastard or Trollope, while others have found it all too much and have changed to something altogether safer and more anonymous. You might like to collect unusual or embarrassing surnames as your researches proceed, just for the fun of it; two favourites from my own collection are John Buffoon (Virginia land patents and grants, 1694) and Robert Plonker (Surrey Musters, 1596: Cattishill).

Name-changers have to be careful not to escape from the frying pan, only to find themselves in the fire: in one well-attested case, a man changed his name to a telephone number because he was lonely, only to find that the bank wouldn't give him a cheque book as his signature was too easily forged . . .

Professor Nicholas Christenfeld, a psychologist from California (where else?) recently conducted a study which concluded that an embarrassing surname can shorten your life. Not only that, but having scrutinised no fewer than five million [sic] death certificates, the Professor found that people with initials like *DUD* or *ILL* died more than seven years earlier than those with initials like *WIN* or *WOW*. Reporting these world-shattering findings in the *Sunday Times* 'Style' section (30th July 2000), Roland White couldn't resist sharing with us a couple of examples of his own: he tells us that he was at school with a girl called Penny Stamp, who didn't find her name at all unusual, and asks us to spare a thought for Rosie Paton of Spalding in Lincolnshire, who married a man called Bottom and so became Rosie Bottom. Retaining her maiden name in a double-barrelled form proved to be no solution – I mean, who wants to be Rosie Paton-Bottom?

To avoid persecution

Finding yourself mocked or taunted because of your surname is one thing; to be severely persecuted because that name reveals something about your family origins is quite another.

To bear a German-sounding name in Britain before and during the First World War could be a recipe for disaster, and many families chose to change their surname as a result. Christopher Degenhardt from Wolfhagen, Hesse via Hamburg, had settled in England in 1859 and was naturalised in 1887; as the new century dawned his two sons, Walter Degenhardt and Frederick Charles Degenhardt, a London shopkeeper, adopted English-sounding alternative surnames, becoming 'Walter Hart'

Changing a German surname for an English one. *Frederick Charles Degenhardt is shown outside his North London shop at 88 St James Road, Holloway, early in the 20th century, alongside his brother Walter Christian Degenhardt. Frederick had decided that it would be prudent to abandon his German surname, and traded simply as 'F. Charles & Co'. (From a photograph kindly provided by Christine Selby of Leigh-on-Sea, Essex)*

and 'Frederick Charles' (his first two names) respectively. Only their elder brother Christopher, a draper living in Dorking, refused to be anything other than a Degenhardt (Christine Selby, *FTM*, August 1994).

Watch out in particular for this ploy of turning a middle name into a surname – one adopted by my hairdresser in Ilkeston, Derbyshire, who has dropped his surname for professional purposes and is known simply as 'Peter James'. Many customers wouldn't even suspect that this wasn't his full name.

To give a boost to a stage or screen career

Many individuals who have aspired to become famous on stage or screen have invented attractive-sounding aliases for themselves, as the following did: William Pratt became Boris Karloff, Marion Michael Morrison became John Wayne, Reginald Truscott-Jones became Ray Milland, Harry Webb became Cliff Richard, and Madonna Louise Veronica Cicone became, simply, Madonna.

Sam Goldwyn of Metro-Goldwyn-Meyer stepped off the boat when he arrived in America and was called Goldfish, a direct translation of his Russian surname. Going into business later with a man called Selwyn, he decided to combine both names. The first permutation, Selfish, had an unfortunate ring about it, so he settled for Goldwyn instead.

There is one example in very recent times of a name-change process which has a rather chilling circularity to it. Farookh Bulsara, born in Zanzibar in 1946, changed his name to Freddie Mercury and became the lead singer in the well-known band, 'Queen'. Charismatic above the ordinary, Freddie inspired a good many imitators and worshippers, one of whom, Barry Michael George of Fulham in London, changed his name to 'Bulsara' – not Freddie's stage name, but the original surname which he had abandoned as he rose to stardom. In February 2001 Barry Michael George, alias Bulsara, appeared in court at the Old Bailey in London, accused of the murder of the much-loved English television presenter, Jill Dando, who had been shot dead on her doorstep in Fulham on 26th April 1999.

To comply with the terms of a will

Members of the nobility or the gentry have not been averse to changing their surname completely if an inheritance was involved: only in this way have various eminent family names not disappeared for lack of male heirs.

I once bought a number of books which bore the fine pictorial bookplate of a gentleman by the name of 'F.A. Page-Turner'. It was some while before I realised that this was one and the same man as F.A. Blaydes, the well-known Bedfordshire genealogist and antiquary. Blaydes had changed his surname to Page-Turner by Royal Licence in 1903, having succeeded to the estates and the baronetcy of his maternal uncle, Sir Edward Henry Page-Turner.

A famous herald at the College of Arms, G.E. Cockayne, had started life as George Adams before assuming his mother's maiden name as his own surname in 1873 in accordance with a wish expressed in her will, and Florence Nightingale's father, William Edward Shore, abandoned his own surname and became 'Nightingale' in 1815 on inheriting the Derbyshire estates of his mother's uncle, Peter Nightingale.

If you need help in unearthing surname changes of this kind, you should refer to *An index to changes of name under authority of Act of Parliament or Royal Licence and including irregular changes from I George III to 64 Victoria, 1760 to 1901* by W.P.W. Phillimore and E.A. Fry, 1905 (reprinted Baltimore, 1968).

Turning the page. *When the Bedfordshire genealogist F.A. Blaydes inherited the baronetcy and the estates of his maternal uncle, he changed his surname to 'Page-Turner' by Royal Licence. This book-plate was engraved for him by F.V. Hadlow in 1908.*

> Extract from
>
> The Parish Registers of
> St Bartholomew the Less, London
> a.d. 154⁷⁄₈ to 1812 -
>
> made by me in Nov. & Dec. 1859.
>
> G.E. Adams
>
> Yours most sincerely
> George E Cokayne

Mummy says I should change my surname. *In 1859 the eminent genealogist, George Edward Cockayne, was still calling himself 'G.E. Adams'. By the time he signed his name to a letter on 5th April 1887, however, he had officially acquired the new surname of Cockayne, in accordance with a wish expressed in his mother's will.*

HAR] *An Index to Changes of Name.* 147

Hancock *see* Liebenrood.
Hancorn *see* Duppa.
Handasyde *see* Sharp-Handasyde.
Handforde-Drinkwater : Drinkwater, J., late of Duckinfield, Cheshire, now of Richmond Villa, Redhill, Surrey, gent. Times, 23 Sept., 1871.
Handley *see* Davenport-Handley.
Hand-Newton : Hand, N. D. 18 April, 1806 (511).
Handy-Church : Handy, Maj. 15 Oct., 1832 (2371).
Hanford : Hanford-Flood, J. C. 6 March, 1893 (1540).
Hanford-Flood : Lloyd-Flood, W. 4 June, 1861 (2575).
Hanham *see* Swinburne-Hanham.
Hankey *see* Alers-Hankey.
Hankin, Hy. A. Trulock : Hankin, H. A., of 116, Church Road, Canonbury. Times, d.p., 28 Sept., 1876.
　　see Turvin.
Hanmer *see* Hervey.
Hannam-Clark : Clark, F., of Queen Street, Glos., solicitor. Times, d.p., 31 Jan., 1889.
Hanning *see* Lee.
Hanning-Lee : Lee, E. H., of Bighton, Hants, Lieut. 2nd Life Guards. Times, d.p., 13 June, 1876.
Hansard : Yockney, V. H. 8 July, 1898 (4274).
Hanson : Kershaw, W. B. 20 June, 1844 (2133).
　　see Lucas.
Hanson-Inglish : Hanson, B. 3 May, 1800 (423).
　　　　　　　: Hanson, B. 26 Dec., 1834 (2).
Hanson Torriano : Hanson, L. L., of Ryde, I.W., widow. Times, d.p., 29 April, 1875.
Hanway : Balack, H. 15 July, 1775 (11578).
Harcourt, Francis Vernon : Harcourt, Francis Geo. Randolph, of Buxted Park, Carlton Gdns., and St. Clare, I.W., Col. Times, 1 Jan., 1874.
　　　　: Harcourt-Ainslie, G. S. 15 Feb., 1823 (251).
　　　　: Masters, C. H. 20 March, 1810 (407).
　　　　: Vernon, Rt. Hon. E. V. 15 Jan., 1831 (123).
Hardcastle *see* Burghardt-Hardcastle.
　　　,, Smith Hardcastle.
Hardie *see* Daniel.
Harding *see* Duffield-Harding.
　　,, Emmerson-Harding.
　　: Harding-Featherstone, R. 26 May, 1853 (1665).
　　see Hardinge.
　　E. W. *see* Jefferson-Conkling, P.
　　see Newman.
　　,, Nott.

Printed index of name changes. *In 1905 W.P.W. Phillimore and E.A. Fry published a useful work entitled* An index to changes of name under authority of Act of Parliament or Royal Licence and including irregular changes from I George III to 64 Victoria, 1760 to 1901.

Other reasons

Another very simple reason for a surname change is revealed in the writings of the 19th-century diarist, Francis Kilvert, who lived and worked on the Welsh-English border:

> *Thursday 12th February 1874. Visited old John Bryant. The Patriarch was snugly ensconced in bed like a marmot in his burrow. He said he meant to stay there during the cold weather. He told me his real name is John Jeffries, but he was always called Bryant because, his father and mother being dead, he was brought up by his Bryant grandfather and grandmother. He was about 94 years old at the time.* (F. Cook, *FTM*, June 1995)

How to change a surname

How do surnames become changed? Traditionally this would be by way of an Act of Parliament or by Royal Licence, though most people are more familiar with the idea of a change by Deed Poll; such official alterations were entered on the Close Rolls until 1903, and thereafter in the Enrolment Books of the Supreme Court. When such books are more than three years old, they are deposited at the Public Record Office in class J18. Between 1939 and 1945 British subjects could only change their name if they published a notice of such intent in the *London Gazette* or in its Scottish or Irish equivalents.

It's all very well to make an official statement of the fact that you wish to change your surname in this way, but what really counts is everyday usage. Legally it is your baptismal name that defines you as the person you are; it can only be changed by an Act of Parliament, by a Bishop at a confirmation service or by a name being added on adoption. The good news is that if you weren't baptised, you can call yourself what you like! Your surname, by contrast, is simply an 'added' name and – oddly enough – you can change it at will, simply by announcing the fact that henceforward you wish to be known as Fred Nerk, not as Fred Bloggs. The Master of the Rolls said in 1730 that he was 'satisfied that anyone may take upon him what surname and as many surnames as he pleases', and in 1822 Lord Chief Justice Abbot added: 'A name assumed by the voluntary act of a man adopted by all who know him and by which he is constantly called, becomes as much and as effectively his name as if he had obtained an Act of Parliament to confer it upon him.' (Quotations taken from Pauline Litton's 'Topical Tips', *FTM*, January 2001.)

Nicknames

**Don't be surprised to find that your ancestor was known by a nickname

It's a fact of life that we are all known by a number of different names in varying circumstances. Mr Thomas Smith might respond to being called 'Mr Smith', 'T. Smith Esquire', 'Sir', 'Thomas', 'Tom', 'Dad', 'Grandad', 'Darling', 'Pet' – or even, 'Oi, YOU!'

Sometimes even this range of possibilities is insufficient, and individuals acquire a nickname. Traditionally people with the surname White would be referred to as 'Chalky'; the surname Williams will often give rise to 'Bill' as a nickname, regardless of the person's real first name, and if your name is Tony and your little sister could never quite get her tongue around this when she was very young, you might become 'Tototo', reflecting her best shot at it. A plaintive comment on this state of affairs comes from W. Somerset Maugham:

> *I christened her 'Maria del Sol', because she was my first child and I dedicated her to the glorious sun of Castille; but her mother calls her 'Sally', and her brother, 'Pudding Face'.*

The use of nicknames appears to be a fairly universal practice. Peter Spear (*FTM*, April 1994) came across a fascinating example from the records of Blood Indian Reserve, Cardston, Alberta, Canada: 'The Riflewoman or Nostrils or Mary Ironpipe, born 1857, daughter of Ironpipe and Ugly Looking Woman.' Just how rare or common these names would prove to be could only be determined, of course, if we knew just how many Ugly-Looking Women and the rest there were on the reserve at the time …

A nickname might be added to an existing first name ('Red Jack Thompson') or it might replace it ('Red Thompson'). As a family historian you may have a real challenge when trying to determine the identity of a person bearing a nickname, or you may not even suspect that one was being used. A classic story along these lines appeared in *Family Tree Magazine*, May 2000, submitted by Laurie Lay but originally featured in *Cassel's Illustrated Family Paper* (16th August 1862):

> *Every man in the colliery (Staffordshire) bears a personal sobriquet, descriptive of some peculiarity, but scarcely any person goes by his family name. A story is told of an attorney's clerk who was employed to serve a process on one of these oddly-named persons. The clerk, after a great deal of*

*enquiry as to the whereabouts of the party, was about to
abandon the search as hopeless, when a young woman kindly
volunteered to assist him.*
*'Oy say, Bullyed,' cried she to the first person they met, 'does
thee know a man called Adam Green?' The bull-head was
shaken in token of ignorance. Then they came to another man.
'Lay-a-bed, dost thee?' Lie-a-bed could not answer either.
'Stumpy' (a man with a wooden leg), 'Cowskin', 'Spindle-
shanks', 'Cock-eye' and 'Pigtail' were successively consulted,
but to no purpose. At length, however, having had conversa-
tion with several friends, the damsel's eye suddenly brigh-
tened, and slapping one of her neighbours upon the shoulder,
she exclaimed, 'Dash my wig! Whey he means mey feyther!'
Then turning to the astonished clerk, she cried, 'You should'n
ax'd for Olde Blackbird!' So it appeared that the old miner's
name, though he was a man of substance, was not known even
to his own daughter.*

John Cooper (*FTM*, January 1995) was never very pleased to have an
unusual middle name, 'Binham' (his great grandmother's maiden
name), especially when kids, being kids, used this as a nickname for
him as soon as they noticed his embarrassment about it. This was at
Withernsea High School in East Yorkshire. John's sister was then
dubbed 'Binham's Lass', his younger brother became 'Little Binham'
and his youngest sister 'Binham's Little Lass'. John's attitude to all this
has since changed: he is now proud of his middle name – and quite right,
too!

The father of Mary Wilks of Winchester (*FTM*, April 1993) was
always known by the nickname of 'Ronald' Garland, and appeared as
such on his death certificate, though his real name was William E.G.
Garland. Mary tried to persuade the registration authorities to add a
marginal note of explanation to the certificate, but without success. My
paternal grandfather, registered at birth as *Henry* Titford, but always
known as *Harry*, was luckier. His marriage certificate of 1902 was
modified 46 years after the event, to allow him to inherit a modest
legacy from his brother. A marginal note was added: 'In entry no.6, col.2
for 'Harry' read 'Henry (or Harry)' '.

Christine Selby of Leigh-on-Sea in Essex tells me that her mother was
christened 'Agnes Elisabeth Degenhardt' in 1899. Now we have seen
already that one of the Degenhardts changed his surname to 'Charles'
early in the 20th century, so Agnes Elisabeth was a 'Charles' by the time
she went to school. So far so good – but Agnes's father always referred
to her as his little 'sunbeam' – a name which stuck, so she was always
known as 'Beam Charles' to family and friends alike. Agnes Degenhardt

alias Beam Charles died at Rayleigh in Essex in 1983, by which time no one was aware of her baptismal name or her German origins. Tracking down the ancestry of someone whose name has changed so completely should keep you on your genealogical toes!

There will be communities even to this day where there is a need to distinguish individuals because one surname is so widespread. In a Scottish village full of 'James MacKay's, or in a Welsh settlement bristling with 'Hugh Williams's, nicknames will be employed in the interests of precision – hence 'Jones the coal', 'Evans the bread' and the like. And this doesn't apply only in Scotland and Wales ... Mrs Rhoda Windiate-Blackmore (*FTM*, September 1994) has ancestors from Brightling, Sussex, surnamed Relf. The rector's so-called 'Parish Business' ledger dating from 1850–60 contains a long list of those receiving beef and bread at Christmas, 1850, including Thomas 'Squat' Relf, Thomas 'Smother' Relf, Thomas 'Lame' Relf, Thomas 'Keeper' Relf, Thomas 'Bully' Relf and Thomas 'Brick' Relf. It's lucky that each man had at least something distinctive about him upon which to hang a nickname!

Sometimes an entire family branch will be known by a separate nickname to distinguish it from others with the same surname. This is certainly the case within the hamlet of Cotmanhay, Ilkeston, Derbyshire, where the surnames Beardsley and Henshaw preponderate. Anyone announcing the fact that his or her name is Henshaw can expect those in the know to ask, 'Are you one of the *Bod-Tod* 'Enshaws?' Just how unsavoury such a nickname is, I leave readers with some feeling for the dialect to determine.

It is certainly true, of course, that a number of present-day surnames are themselves derived from a nickname used by or about a distant ancestor many hundreds of years ago, reflecting his looks, figure, temperament, and so on: *Redhead* (red haired); *Tench* (fat and sleek, like the fish); *Trueman* (trusty and faithful); *Bragge* (proud, arrogant, brisk, brave).

**Be on the look-out for hereditary nicknames

One phenomenon which may worry family historians if they ever stumble across it, is that even in recent times there have been some communities in which nicknames themselves are hereditary, passed on from one generation to the next. This is certainly true of a number of fishing communities, and Norman Holding, writing to *Family Tree Magazine* in April 1994, refers to the practice as used in Leigh-on-Sea, Essex. Here nicknames were in regular use as early as 1820, and many were in fact inherited. John 'Tolley' Cotgrove would be known purely as 'Tolley', not even as 'Tolley Cotgrove' in full, and his son William

Cotgrove became 'Billy Tolley'. Similarly, William Cotgrove was 'Lumpy', later 'Old Lump'; his son George became 'George Lump', and his grandson Bert gloried in the name 'Bert Lump'. This may have been a canny ruse developed by a close-knit community in order to confuse customs officials and other snoopers, but how unfair it now seems to present-day family historians!

There are certainly examples of nicknames being used on official documents. Stanley Riley (*FTM*, August 1994) makes reference to the fishing community of North Meols, Southport, Lancashire, where William 'Cotty' Wright of Marshside, North Meols, tanner, describes himself precisely in this way in his will of 1854, and makes his signature accordingly. In the apportionment relating to the tithe map for North Meols (1839/40) the occupiers were named, and in brackets after common names came trade (fisherman, publican, etc); district of abode (South Hawes, Rowe Lane, etc); possessive male Christian name (presumably of father); possessive female Christian name (presumably of mother, or perhaps wife) – and nickname (Catty, Fiddlers, Cotty, Bint, etc). The nickname 'Catty' was applied only to Rimmer and Ball, and 'Cotty' only to Wright. It can be a complicated matter! John Bartlett of Stalham, Norfolk, meanwhile (*FTM*, August 1994) tells us that the burial register of Sturminster Newton, Dorset, has an entry which reads: *Mary Bartlett, St.Mar., 6 Feb. 1858, aged 72, 'Her husband was called by the people, "Shongo"'*. (Wright's *Dialect Dictionary* gives the meaning of 'Shongo' as 'A handful of corn' – not so very complimentary ...)

First Names

**Be on the lookout for first-name variants

Funny old things, first names. We have seen already that many surnames have developed and changed over time, and that you can change yours if you wish, but by and large people like to keep their surnames intact, unaltered. Not so with first names. There are time-honoured tailor-made variations on most male and female first names – over 200 for the name 'Elizabeth' alone – not to mention those that individuals can dream up for themselves. I once asked the eminent archivist F.G. Emmison why he was called 'Derick' (not 'Derek'), when his initials were 'F.G.'. He kindly and patiently pointed out to me that 'Derick' was simply a component in his first name, 'Fre*derick*'.

It really is essential to be aware of as many established first-name variations as possible:

> *Ann* can be *Nancy* or *Nanny*
> *Beatrice* can be *Trixie*

Mary can be *Molly* or *Polly*
Frances can be *Fanny*
Sarah can be *Sally*
Elizabeth can be *Elisabeth, Bess, Bessy, Beth, Betsy, Betty,*
    Elsbeth, Elsie, Eliza, Libby, Lisa, Liza, Liz, Lizzy –
    and many others
Henry can be *Harry*
Lawrence can be *Larry*
Richard can be *Dick*
William can be *Bill*
Herbert can be *Bert*

And so on . . .

It took me quite a while, when following a family line back into the late 16th century, to realise that a lady whose first name was 'Matilda' was the same person as one being referred to as 'Maud'. Initially I had the same person marked on the pedigree as two separate individuals!

Luckily help is at hand here, in the shape of an excellent book which includes a dictionary-style listing, called *First name variants* by Alan Bardsley, published by the Federation of Family History Societies in 1996 (2nd edition). This should answer most of your questions.

**Consider that a person may have changed his or her first name

We have seen that legally your baptismal name is more difficult to change than your surname, but we must all know people who have rejected their original first name and replaced it with one they preferred. I have a friend who was christened Theodore Robert; his mother called him 'Theo', his friends knew him as 'Robert', but when he was at Medical School in London he decided that he wished to be known as 'Simon' – and he has been 'Dr. Simon Bailey' throughout his professional career. It is not at all uncommon to find that a person prefers to be known by the second of his or her given names, rather than the first. So it is that the politicians James Harold Wilson and John Enoch Powell were only ever known in public life as 'Harold' and 'Enoch'.

Speaking of Enoch . . . Celia Williams wrote to *Family Tree Magazine* in June 1995 to say that an old friend of hers who was in service many years ago had had to change his name in a flash from 'Enoch' to 'Ted' when a prospective employer flatly refused to employ anyone called 'Enoch'. Celia also pointed out, very pertinently for family historians, that you may have failed to identify a servant ancestor as a result of the common practice in times past of calling every successive maid, 'tweeny' or footman in the household by the same first name, regardless of the individual's real name. The master or mistress of the house might take the view that their parlour maid was always Eliza, the tweeny was always Sarah, and the footman was always George. So beware!

In a few unfortunate cases, infants have had their names changed for them inadvertently even at the time of baptism. It seems that fathers were quite likely to be the guilty parties in such instances. In July 1994 Mrs Brenda Ball wrote to *Family Tree Magazine* with a transcript of an entry from the parish register of Holy Trinity, Hull (original spellings retained):

> *1770. Baptism. Mary daughter of Thomas Hewson. N.B. Mr Hewson gave the child's name Charlotte. And he his the eleventh father whom we have found giving there childrens name wrong at the 'Font' in 8 years, and there are many children registered by the wrong name in the register books. Query, whether these mistakes have arisen from the cause above, or neglect of clerk who is generally blamed in those cases, or whether it would not be better that every parent should give it in writing. Thos Fletcher [signed]*

Giving a child's baptismal name in writing? A good idea, we may say – if only every parent could write!

**Look at first names very carefully: do they offer any useful clues in their own right?

Classically-minded families were wont to give various of their children a first name which placed him or her precisely in the brotherly or sisterly sequence. Tertius Lydgate, the ambitious young doctor in George Eliot's novel *Middlemarch*, was no doubt the third son of his parents, and you might encounter seventh sons called Septimus or eighth sons called Octavius, even if it's on somebody else's family tree. This was mainly a male phenomenon, though some girls baptised Octavia may well have been the eighth in line. A child born during the Christmas season, of course, was quite likely to attract the name of Noel or Noele.

If your family tree features a man called Charles or James, born at the time of the English Civil War or during the interregnum which followed, you can be fairly certain that the family's loyalties lay with the Royalists, these being the names of Stuart kings. If, on the other hand, you have ancestors in more recent times with names like Ebenezer or Kezia – as I do – then gentle but persistent alarm bells should start ringing immediately. These are the kind of names favoured by non-conformists, dating originally from a Puritan practice which began in the 1560s, following the publication of the Geneva Bible. Many a dissenter thereafter, it is said, would rather stick a pin into an open copy of the Old Testament to find a name for a new-born child than have recourse to the Saints' names so favoured by Roman Catholics.

Are there 'Selina's in your family? *Many families named a daughter 'Selina' in honour of Selina Hastings, Countess of Huntingdon (1707–1791), an influential non-conformist and friend of John Wesley.* [Reproduced from a photograph kindly supplied by The Building of Bath Museum]

Another name with a strong non-conformist flavour is Selina. This was the Christian name of Selina Hastings, Countess of Huntingdon (1707–91), a great friend of John Wesley, who founded a Calvinistic sect which was named after her. It is probable, though not certain, that any ancestor of yours named Selina came from a Methodist family, or more specifically from one which belonged to the so-called Lady Huntingdon's Connexion.

Ebenezer is a standard enough Old Testament name, and many non-conformists use it in the title of their chapels. Keziah was the name given by Job to the second of his daughters; when I discovered that a great-grandmother of mine had this as a middle name, I thought what a relief it was that she hadn't been named after Job's third daughter, Karenhappuch, which hardly trips easily off the tongue. I needn't have worried. Colin Mangham from Bury in Lancashire wrote to *Family Tree Magazine* in May 1994 to ask if readers could help explain the middle names of two of the sons of Ebenezer Shaw, cordwainer, and his wife Ann, who were baptised at Swinton, Yorkshire, in 1838 and 1840 respectively: William *Mahershalalhashbaz* Shaw and John *Zerubbabel* Shaw. The Magazine's readers, as ever, were up to the task. Mahershalalhashbaz, it seems, was a symbolic name given to a son of Isaiah, and one man of the name of Zerubbabel was a descendant of a King of Judah, while another was the son of Pedaiah, brother of Shimei. Tom Robinette wrote to say that his family, which is of Huguenot descent, had had the name Zorabable, spelled at times as Zorababel or Zerobabel, in continuous use from the early 18th century to the present day. I must say that Kezia and Karenhappuch seem like positively ordinary names compared to these, but the last word on the subject came from Arthur Royall, who was happy to quote a tale from *The Norfolk Diary* by Benjamin Armstrong, vicar of Dereham:

> *25 Dec. 1867. Married a young parishioner of the name of Mahershalalhashbaz. He accounted for the possession of so extraordinary a name thus: his father wished to call him by the shortest name in the bible, and for that purpose selected 'Uz'. But the clergyman making some demur, the father said in pique, 'Well if he cannot have the shortest, he shall have the longest'.*

Fans of unusual non-conformist naming practices should lose no time in reading an entertaining book by C.W. Bardsley, called *Curiosities of Puritan nomenclature* (1880). Here you will find all the old favourites, such as the 17th-century anabaptist, leather-seller and politician called 'Praise-God' Barbone (or Barbones) and his brothers 'Christ came into the world to save sinners' Barbon and 'If Christ had not died thou hadst been damned' Barbon. The latter, sad to relate, was referred to by his detractors simply as 'Damned Barbon'. And I wonder how 'Remember-death Cowper', baptised in 1620 at St Michael's, Sittingbourne, Kent, was known by those who wished to take him down a peg or two? (Peter Mills, *FTM*, June 1993).

C.W. Bardsley, not content with having written a book on Puritan nomenclature and a well-known dictionary of surnames, was also a great collector of unusual first names, several of which are featured in his book *English Surnames: their sources and significations* (1906):

Above-town, Beneath-the-town, Blackinthemouth, Bloodletter, Blisswench, Cheese-and-bread, Cock's brains, Fresherring, From-above, Glossycheek, Go-in-the-wind, Halfnaked, Hatechrist, Hell-cat, Holy-water-clerk, Jackanapes, Leave-to-day, Mildew, Ninepence, Nose, Onehand, Perfect-sparrow, Pudding, Rattlebag, Shave-tail, Shunchrist, Speaklittle, Sweat-in-bed, Weaslehead, Whelk, and Without-the-town.

Puritan zealots were not alone in having burdened their children with a set of convoluted first names. It is not unknown in recent times for infants to be given the surnames of a successful football team to carry with them through life as a set of first names, and broadcaster, musician and family historian Steve Race wrote to *Family Tree Magazine* in November 1998 to recount the story of French conductor and composer Louis Jullien (1812–1860), whose baptism was sponsored by 35 members of the local philharmonic society, each of whom chose a Christian name for him, poor soul. The name Joseph cropped up twice (albeit hyphenated to another name), and Thomas three times.

John P.G. Fysh of Croydon also wrote to say that he had seen a chilling headline in the *Daily Telegraph* during November 1986: 'Baby to keep 140 names'. A couple from Chesterfield, Derbyshire, had chosen this 140-strong collection for their daughter, and had faced (not surprisingly) a long-fought battle with officialdom over the birth certificate. In the end a compromise was reached: the surname would be on the certificate, and the first names on a separate document.

Spare a thought, also, for the daughter of Arthur Pepper (laundry proprietor) and his wife Sarah Jane, born in West Derby, Lancashire, in 1882 and named: Ann Bertha Cecilia Diana Emily Fanny Gertrude Hypatia Inez Jane Kate Louise Maud Nora Ophelia Quince Rebecca Starkey Teresa Ulysis Venus Winifred Xenophon Yetty Zeus. This is a full house: one first name beginning with each letter of the alphabet in turn, leaving out the letter 'P' because that is the first letter of the surname. (G.A. Foster, *FTM*, January 1995). It was delightful to read in *Family Tree Magazine* (April 1995) that Phoebe Kemp from the Wirral was distantly related to Ann Bertha Cecilia (etc) Pepper and that the poor girl was known simply as 'A.B.C. Pepper'. How charming! One of Phoebe's cousins used to recite all of A.B.C.'s names as a party piece!

There really does seem to be no end to the insensitivity of some parents when it comes to bestowing first names upon their hapless children. There are well-attested examples of boys being called Judas and Cain, and in 1842 Samuel and Sophia Thomson presented their son for baptism in Burwash, Sussex, requesting that he be named 'Oranges and lemons'. The clergyman objected, and a compromise of 'Samuel Orange' was arrived at.

In more recent times, *The Observer* newspaper for 1st May 1994 reported that one hapless vicar was asked to baptise a child 'Delboy', after the star of the television series, *Only fools and horses*, while another balked at being asked by a couple in Buxted, East Sussex, to name their child 'Beelzebub'. It almost beggars belief.

The Thurston family of Michigan in the USA were not much kinder to their children, naming them Ulysses Ithicus, Leodia Iphigenia, Chrystemas Andromea, Epimondas Epaphroditus, Achilles Lycurgus, Militiades Aristiades, Cassius Brutus, Solon Kossuth, Agathemnon Hiland, Dulcena Dulcerado, Patroclas Antilocus and (very ordinary, this) Wendell Phillips. For some reason this little American saga was reported in *The Newbury [Berkshire] News*, 4 June 1868, and was submitted to *Family Tree Magazine* by Julie Goddard in September 1999.

The Welsh can play a similar game, it seems. The following examples of bizarre names given by John and Lavinia Rebecca Turner to their offspring, taken from the bishop's transcripts for Mold, Flintshire, were sent to *Family Tree Magazine* in February 1995 by Elizabeth Pritchard of Aberystwyth:

> *Cornelius La Compston Turner* and *Bernard de Belton Turner*, baptised 1838; *Turnerica Henrica Ulrica Da Gloria De Lavinia Rebecca Turner*, buried 1840; *Hillgrave de John Turner*, baptised 1841; *Eginhard de George Turner Jones Turner*, baptised 1844.

The only good news here, I guess, is that you'd know you had the correct Turner if you were searching for one of these. I mean, how many Turnerica Henrica Ulrica Da Glorida De Lavinia Rebecca Turners have there ever been throughout recorded history, do you think?

How about having an ancestor named Sir Richard Carew Percival? You won't find him in any books on baronets or knights, alas, as he appears to have acquired 'Sir' as a form of Christian name when he was born in South Norwood in 1862. Sir Richard's grand-daughter, Shelagh

Worsell of Bournemouth (*FTM*, July 1994), has traced her Percival ancestry to Lincolnshire in 1712 – but has found no sign of any real titles in the family. Good luck to Sir Richard, I say – he can join the ranks of Duke Ellington and Count Basie – not to mention the redoubtable Earl Gillette of razor fame.

As it happens, Sir Percival is out-ranked by other commoners with grand names, such as Prince Edward Fergus O'Connor Squire Wood, son of plain 'John Wood' (baptised at Wakefield parish church in 1885) and – a wonderful example of *lèse majesté* – King Reeson (baptised on 5th January 1823 at Leake in Lincolnshire). King reigned until 1891, when he died in Lambeth (Irene Burton and Mrs Linda Bridges [née Reeson], *FTM*, January 1995).

It's not always the parents' fault. There have been times when individuals have voluntarily lumbered themselves with less-than-conventional first names. Fenella Smith of Stouffville, Ontario, was kind enough to write to me in 1994 to share an item from the *Toronto Sun* of 25th April of that year, featuring 17 year old Peter Eastman of Santa Barbara, California, who appeared in court in order to register his new name. Henceforth he would be known as 'Trout Fishing in America' – taken, you understand, from a 1967 novel of the same name by Richard Brautigan. 'Most people say it's a cool thing,' said the articulate Trout. 'It's just breaking away. I'm just saying, "I am not this little kid any more. I am my own person".' Having lived in San Francisco for a year (and a very wonderful place it is, too), I thought that nothing could surprise me, until I read this. Trout's father, by the way, was happy to fork out the $182 filing fee for the new name. He is very much in favour of having a son who is his own person, it seems.

**Don't always assume that a person is male or female based upon first-name evidence alone

Mrs Barbara Armitage wrote to *Family Tree Magazine* in July 1995 to share with us a passage from that wonderful book *The common stream* by Rowland Parker, an in-depth history of a Cambridgeshire village which is a classic of its kind and a model to others:

> *Was it pure benevolence which prompted [John Welbore] to leave 'to Wendy Oxford and Philip Oxford £3 6s 8d a piece towards their being put out as apprentice'?*

You might have thought, as I did, that Wendy Oxford is a delightful name for a girl. Think again! The future apprentice featured here was a boy, whose first name was derived from an eminent family named 'Wendy' who lived at Haslingfield. As it happens, the popular theory that the girl's name Wendy was invented out of a clear blue sky by J.M. Barrie for use in *Peter Pan* (1904), based upon the daughter of a friend of his who used to call him her 'Friendy Wendy', had already been dealt a severe blow by an 1841 census entry for Bedminster, Bristol, unearthed by Jane Baker: here was a 15 year old girl called Wendy Brookman, daughter of Benjamin Brookman, a butcher, living at 6 Spring Street. (Jane Baker, *FTM*, January 1995).

The name Wendy, it would seem from the above evidence, may have followed the same route as the name Shirley: starting life as a surname, it then became a first name for boys, then for girls. Sometimes it is clear when a surname is being used as a first name, but often enough the surname used in this way masquerades as a familiar first name in its own right.

Do be cautious, then, about ascribing a gender to an individual you come across in your research. Mrs J.B. Mellor of Chingford, writing to *Family Tree Magazine* in September 1994, reported that she had found a male ancestor with the forename 'Beryl'. So be warned!

Even in recent times I have been surprised – perhaps I shouldn't have been – by coming across a boy with the predominantly female first name of 'Tracey', and certainly names like Hilary or Kim can happily be given to male or female offspring alike. Sometimes the only distinction between a male and a female name is the spelling: in principle Francis is male, while Frances is female; Leslie is male, but Lesley is female. Don't depend upon this distinction being rigidly adhered to, however, especially with the name Francis/Frances.

It always gives me food for thought to contemplate that in the

---

FamilySearch™ International Genealogical Index v4.01   British Isles

IGI Record

Select record to download - (50 maximum)

☐ **Francis PARKES**
  Sex: M

Marriage(s):
  Spouse: Frances PARKES
  Marriage: 30 Dec 1849
              Alfreton, Derby, England

'**I, Francis, take thee, Frances to be my lawful wedded wife** ...' *It seems unnecessarily thoughtless of Francis Parkes to have muddied the genealogical waters by marrying a lady by the name of Frances Parkes at Alfreton in Derbyshire in 1849. (From the on-line version of the Church of Jesus Christ of Latter-day Saints'* International Genealogical Index, *at www.familysearch.org)* [Reprinted by permission. Copyright © 1980, 1999, by Intellectual Reserve Inc.]

Derbyshire village in which we live there has been at least one occasion on which a Francis Parkes (male) has married another Frances Parkes (female). Cousin marriages and similar first names – a trap for the unwary ...

There are examples of males being given female names (and vice versa) at the font, be it by design or by accident:

> *Thomas, son of Thomas Messenger and Elizabeth his wife, was born and baptized Oct.24, 1731, by the midwife at the font, called a boy, and named by the godfather, Thomas, but proved a girl!!* (Parish register, Hanwell, Middlesex).

And wouldn't you be confused to find in your own family history a reference to a lady buried in Shorne, Kent, in 1543, named 'Elisabeth Chapman, Gent'?

**Be open to the possibility that a number of siblings may have been given the same first name

One of the great surprises for family historians who have never encountered such a thing before is the fact that a number of parents in centuries past would quite happily give two or more of their surviving children the same first name.

We know this was a common practice when a child died young; parents who lost a son or daughter in childhood would then use the deceased child's name again for subsequent children – in the hope that one, at least, might survive to become an adult. What is more disturbing to the neat mind, however, is to find that the same first name could be repeated even when the original bearer of it was still alive – a practice not uncommon in earlier times, and still occasionally used even into the 18th century and later.

The reasons for this practice can only be guessed at: maybe it looked as if the first child to bear a particular name would die, but he or she didn't, after all; maybe the family were unduly fond of a name and wished to use it as often as possible – or maybe they wished to perpetuate the name of a favourite relative and adopted a belt and braces (and then some) approach?

Examples are plentiful, but one will suffice here: Thomas Bruster of East Keele in Lincolnshire left a will, proved in 1527, in which he made bequests to 'John Bruster, my eldyst son', but also to 'John Bruster, my youngest sone'. You can imagine the genealogical complications which could arise from such a scenario!

A slightly different story emerges from the parish register of Caldecote in Cambridgeshire (details submitted to *Family Tree*

Magazine, August 2000, by Andy Maltpress):
> Baptised 6 July 1722. Burd, John, Son of Simon and Mary.
> Baptised at home, being not well.
> Buried 8 July 1722. Burd, John, son of Simon and Mary.
> (these two children of master Burd were twins and by a
> mistake were both named alike. He that is set down first, is the
> youngest).

Thank goodness that the parish register gives us this amount of detail! Without it we might have been led a really merry dance.

**Be aware that first names, like surnames, may have been inherited

It can be all too easy to draw up a pedigree for one generation of your ancestors without giving too much thought to the significance of each first-name which is featured, or considering whether any regular patterns of naming might be at work.

Choosing an attractive and appropriate first name for a new-born child has often proved to be a daunting task for parents in recent times. Recourse may be had to First Name Dictionaries, father and mother might disagree over alternatives, and fashion may be taken into account, giving us a generation of girls named after Hayley Mills or – only time will tell – boys called Leo in imitation of Leo Blair, the Prime Minister's son, born in the year 2000.

For many of our ancestors matters were not so complicated. There were fewer acceptable boys' and girls' first names to choose from – though fashions have changed over the centuries – and there would be family expectations about which child was named after which existing family member, ancestor or close friend. In other words, it was unusual for a child to be named on a whim; many first-names borne by our ancestors were inherited, just as their surnames were, though if the reigning Queen was named Victoria or the nation's foremost naval hero was Horatio, we must expect to find families who used such names for their own much more humble offspring.

**Look at middle names very carefully: do they offer any useful clues to ancestry?

It was only towards the middle of the 18th century that the practice of giving a child more than one forename became widespread, and even then the names were frequently chosen with relatives or close friends in mind, not simply plucked at random out of a clear blue sky.

My father, born in 1904, considered that he had been well and truly lumbered with a middle name that he really disliked: Horace. Had his

I name this child/ship/locomotive/pub/street 'Victoria'. *If the reigning monarch is called 'Victoria', we must expect many families to use the same name for their daughters.*

doting parents found this classical name in a book of trendy Christian names? Not so. It was bestowed upon my father in honour of an uncle he had never known – Horace Charles Titford, who had died at the age of eight months in 1877. For all my father's reservations, at least his parents had put some thought into this choice of name.

Most researchers will be familiar with the phenomenon of a family surname being used as a second or third forename, in order to perpetuate a distaff name or to prevent its dying out. My wife's father and brother bear the middle name Wotton, though years of research have failed to uncover any earlier evidence of such a family surname, and my Scottish grandmother and two of her brothers acquired the middle name of Willox – chosen, so it is said, in the hope of inheriting a small fortune from an ancestor of this name. Such aspirations, need it be said, came to naught. Another quaint little habit in my own family was to give a child the surname of some local dignitary as a forename, so *Marwood* James Henry Titford, born in 1882, was named in honour of the vicar of Curry Rivel in Somerset, Rev Charles Marwood Speke Mules. It could have been worse, I suppose: *Mules* Titford might not have survived the teasing of his contemporaries.

Sometimes the fact that a surname has been used as a forename is less than obvious; names like Frederick, Patrick, Samuel and countless others began life as forenames and then became surnames. If they are then used as a forename again for family reasons, the transition might not strike us at once, if at all.

Do pay attention, then, to middle names which have a surname look about them; they might offer a vital clue to ancestry, but don't always assume that they have come from the distaff side of the family – that is, from the maiden name of a woman who married one of your male ancestors.

There could be variations on a theme here. I once set myself the task of tracing the ancestry of a man named Robert Westland Marston, co-author in 1899 of a splendid scholarly history of the town of Ilkeston in Derbyshire, about whose life and origins almost nothing was known. I wondered at once how it might have been that the names *Marston* and *Westland* had become linked; I assumed that Westland might be the name of a female ancestor, but couldn't be sure. All I could do was to have patience, and see what transpired. I traced Robert Westland Marston's pedigree back to Stephen Marston, a Baptist minister born in the 1790s, living at Boston in Lincolnshire. This was disturbing news, in a way, as I couldn't expect Baptist believers to appear with any frequency in baptism and burial records maintained by the Anglican church. I scanned the International Genealogical Index (IGI) in vain for any marriage of a male Marston to a female Westland, but all I could find was the two surnames yoked together in reverse, as it were: a female Marston, Mary, had married a male Westland, John, at Boston in 1775. This was clearly relevant in a general way, but seemed not to be precisely what I was looking for.

The Westland family had long been resident in Boston, and as luck would have it, the Document Collection at the Society of Genealogists

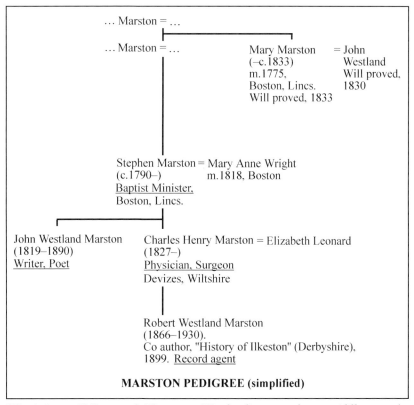

... Marston = ...

... Marston = ...

Mary Marston   = John
(–c.1833)   Westland
m.1775,   Will proved,
Boston, Lincs. 1830
Will proved, 1833

Stephen Marston = Mary Anne Wright
(c.1790–)   m.1818, Boston
Baptist Minister,
Boston, Lincs.

John Westland Marston
(1819–1890)
Writer, Poet

Charles Henry Marston = Elizabeth Leonard
(1827–)
Physician, Surgeon
Devizes, Wiltshire

Robert Westland Marston
(1866–1930).
Co author, "History of Ilkeston" (Derbyshire),
1899. Record agent

MARSTON PEDIGREE (simplified)

What's in a middle name? *The name 'Westland' was used as a middle name by the Marston family in honour of a Westland man who had married a Marston woman and had been a generous benefactor to his Marston in-laws.*

in London had a copy of the will of John Westland of Boston, gentleman, which was made on 19th October 1829, and proved in the Lincoln Consistory Court the following year. Westland was a man of substance who left legacies to a wide variety of people and institutions, including members of the Marston family and Stephen Marston, Baptist minister, in particular. Four years later the will of John Westland's wife Mary was proved; Stephen Marston is again mentioned, this time as her 'nephew', and is named as her executor.

In what way would Stephen Marston be her 'nephew'? A brother's son, a sister's son, or the son of a husband's brother or sister? Not before time, the relevance of the IGI Marston/Westland marriage entry for 1775 dawned upon me, and the fog cleared. John Westland had married

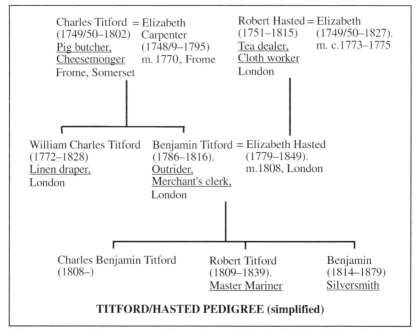

Charles Titford = Elizabeth
(1749/50–1802) Carpenter
Pig butcher, (1748/9–1795)
Cheesemonger m. 1770, Frome
Frome, Somerset

Robert Hasted = Elizabeth
(1751–1815) (1749/50–1827).
Tea dealer, m. c.1773–1775
Cloth worker
London

William Charles Titford
(1772–1828)
Linen draper,
London

Benjamin Titford = Elizabeth Hasted
(1786–1816). (1779–1849).
Outrider, m.1808, London
Merchant's clerk,
London

Charles Benjamin Titford
(1808–)

Robert Titford
(1809–1839).
Master Mariner

Benjamin
(1814–1879)
Silversmith

TITFORD/HASTED PEDIGREE (simplified)

First names used for a reason. *Benjamin and Elizabeth Titford chose their sons' Christian names with care: Charles Benjamin was named after both his paternal grandfather and also his father; Robert was named after his maternal grandfather, and Benjamin was named after his father.*

Mary Marston, and she had a brother (name unknown) who had a son Stephen. So grateful was nephew Stephen for the munificence of his uncle by marriage, that he used the middle name of 'Westland' for one of his sons, John Westland Marston. Not only that, but in 1866 his other son, Charles, passed the same middle name onto his own son, Robert Westland Marston of *History of Ilkeston* fame. 'Westland' was indeed an inherited name, as I had supposed, but it came from a Westland man who had married a Marston lady, not from a Westland lady who had married a Marston man. Keep the thinking flexible!

**Look out for an organised pattern of first-names within a family

I remember the moment when the existence of a regular pattern of first-names in my own male-line ancestry first struck me forcibly out of nowhere, as I sat idly looking at a pedigree I had produced. Charles Titford, pig butcher and cheesemonger of Frome in Somerset, married

Elizabeth Carpenter at the parish church there in 1770. The sons resulting from that marriage were named: William Charles, John, Benjamin and Charles Thynne. Son Benjamin, in turn, married Elizabeth Hasted, daughter of Robert Hasted, in London in 1808, and had sons Charles Benjamin, Robert and Benjamin.

I had never paused to consider whether any kind of regular naming pattern was at work here – what a mistake! Then I thought: 'Why did Benjamin and Elizabeth name their eldest son, baptised at St Mary Whitechapel on 7th April 1808, "Charles Benjamin"?' Well, let's say it was Charles after the paternal grandfather, followed by Benjamin after the father. The second son was called 'Robert', after the maternal grandfather, Robert Hasted. The youngest son was plain 'Benjamin', named after his father.

It was only after I had established this working hypothesis from observable facts that I realised that the family was simply using an ordered system of naming that had been widespread in England up until the 19th century, and one which still prevails in Scotland and elsewhere to this very day.

A baptism at St Mary Whitechapel. *The parish church of St Mary Whitechapel lies in Middlesex, just to the east of the City of London. Charles Benjamin Titford, who was given the Christian names of both his paternal grandfather and his father, was baptised here on 7th April 1808. (From Thomas Shepherd,* London in the nineteenth century, *1827)*

In its simplest form, it works like this:

- The first son is named after the paternal grandfather
- The second son is named after the maternal grandfather
- The third son is named after the father – if this name has not yet been used
- The fourth and any subsequent sons are named after close friends, a favourite relation, or whoever.

The naming of daughters would operate as a satisfying mirror-image of the above:

- The first daughter is named after the maternal grandmother
- The second daughter is named after the paternal grandmother
- The third daughter is named after the mother
- The fourth and subsequent daughters are named after close friends, a favourite relation, or whoever.

There are variations on this theme, and for a very comprehensive survey of the subject you should look at Shirley Hornbeck's web site, 'This and that genealogy tips' (Naming patterns) at http://homepages.rootsweb.com/~hornbeck/naming.htm

In cases where a father died before a male child was born, the son could well be named after him, and similarly when a girl was born to a mother who died in childbirth. A son or daughter born within a second marriage was often named after a deceased husband or wife.

The existence of some kind of ordered first-name system at work in a number of families has several vital implications for our research, of which we may mention three in particular:

● If James and Mary Smith have a number of children, all of whom marry and have children of their own whom they name using a paternal and maternal grandfather system, then an awful lot of these children – first cousins of each other – will also be called James or Mary after the grandparents, and some will also bear the same surname. A simple cry of 'Come in, James, your tea's ready!' could attract half the neighbourhood. It would be in situations such as these, of course, that our old friend the nickname would come into its own, to separate individuals with identical names.

● If anything at all like the naming pattern we have outlined was in operation in your family, you should in theory be able to extrapolate backwards (not half as painful as it sounds). That is, if I had not known that Elizabeth Titford (née Hasted)'s father was named Robert, I could have deduced this crucial fact from the first name given to her second son, Robert Titford. If you haven't ever looked closely for the existence of naming patterns within your own pedigrees, go and do so without delay! You might get some pleasant surprises.

● In principle, a logical naming pattern can enable us to move down a pedigree, forwards in time, as well as up it. An 18th-century ancestor of mine named William, the son of a man of the same name, married and had children. His earliest known son was named Charles, but I was convinced that Charles probably had an older brother, a first-born son named William after his paternal grandfather. Determination to find son William paid off in the long run; not only did I find a record of his existence eventually, but in the process I found his parents living in a place where I would never have dreamed of looking for them.

After all that, a word of warning and of further explanation is called for. I thought I'd be clever and try to apply the naming system I had noted in my own family to try and reach back a further generation, turning to William Charles, John, Benjamin and Charles Thynne, the sons of Charles Titford the cheesemonger of Frome and his wife Elizabeth (née Carpenter). I didn't know (I still don't know!) for certain the names of the parents of Charles or of Elizabeth, but my reasoning went like this: 'If Benjamin Titford of London, son of Charles, baptised his eldest son Charles Benjamin after his father and then himself, surely his elder brother William Charles, son of Charles, must be the grandson of a man called William? Charles the cheesemonger must be the son of William Titford!' It seemed so simple, so obvious – and I wasted a good deal of time over many years, trying to make it true. It now seems almost certain that Charles Titford was in fact the son of a Thomas Titford, not of a William, since there is only evidence for the existence of a Thomas Titford in Frome at the right time – in rentals, Baptist church records, an 18th century census, and so on.

So why 'William Charles'? Here we must refine the system we have outlined. To say that an eldest son was named after his paternal grandfather is only part of the story; in fact what usually happened was that the paternal grandfather would be honoured by being asked to be *godfather* to his eldest grandson. As he acted in this capacity at the font, the child would be named after him. Now in the case of William Charles Titford, son of Charles, the presumed paternal grandfather, Thomas, was dead before William Charles was born; the parents would have had to look elsewhere – in this case, very probably, to Charles the Cheesemonger's elder brother William – for a godfather, and so the child was named after his uncle and father, not after his grandfather and father.

As to William Charles Titford's brothers, we may assume, if we wish, that John was probably named after his maternal grandfather, and little Charles Thynne Titford, who died at the age of eleven months in 1793, was given his middle name in memory of one of his mother's ancestors, 'Thynne Carpenter', who in turn had been named, for some reason not yet established, after the Thynne family, Marquesses of Bath, at Longleat House near Frome.

So it's all very well to have noticed a pattern of naming and to make use of it in order to solve a number of genealogical problems – but once again we must learn the good old trick of flexible thinking if we are not to get hide-bound in our ways. The well-known Norfolk genealogist, Walter Rye, spelt out a timely warning as long ago as 1888 in the first edition of his book, *Records and record searching* (page 5), which still applies today:

> *Never attempt to theorize or speculate too soon. If you get wedded to a theory, you will find yourself unconsciously specially pleading in its favour, and not looking at things fairly.*

Collect unusual names as you go along, just for the fun of it

As your family research progresses, you're almost certain to come across some amusing examples of names: an odd first name, an odd surname, or an odd combination of the two. Such examples probably won't be directly relevant to your own family, so you might be tempted to have a chuckle and then pass on your way. Why not pause for a second? Eccentric names, like other genealogical snippets you might stumble across as you continue your research, are always worth jotting down. Why not keep a small 'commonplace book' in which you record amusing little gems in order to return to them later for the amusement of yourself, your family and your friends? In line with good scholarly practice, do note the precise source of each example you find – just in case you ever need to justify its veracity, or to return to it at a later date. Start with the IGI in your search for oddities, if you like; here you'll soon come across lovely people such as Sarah *Tortoiseshell* and David Perrot *Tortoiseshell*, born in Bridport in Dorset in 1839, and many others.

Some names almost beggar belief. Joyce Dye from Walnut Creek in California wrote to *Family Tree Magazine* in December 1993 to tell us that she had found an infant named Underwriter Daly born on an immigrant ship which arrived in New York in 1851, while Sue Allaby had culled the following genuine specimens of surrealist names whilst trawling through Pigot's 1839 Directory for Kent, Essex and Sussex:

Familysearch® International Genealogical Index™ v4.01	British Isles

IGI Record

Select record to download - (50 maximum)

⌐ **Christmas DAY**
  Sex: M

Event(s):
  Christening: 27 Dec 1762
  Lowestoft, Suffolk, England

Parents:
  Father: Thomas DAY
  Mother: Mary

Happy Christmas! *A number of surnames lend themselves to interesting combinations. Here Thomas Day and his wife Mary are taking their male child, 'Christmas', for baptism on 27th December. Maybe they had arranged it so that he was born on Christmas Day itself? (From the on-line version of the Church of Jesus Christ of Latter-day Saints'* International Genealogical Index, *at:* www.familysearch.org) [Reprinted by permission. Copyright © 1980, 1999, by Intellectual Reserve, Inc.]

Theys Boys Claringbold, Aylee Maas, Loft Raspisou, Bannister Sly, Draper Usmar, N. Icely, Onesiphorous Paul, Breathard Tilmouth and Zaphnathpaaneah Drayson. As tennis-player John McEnroe once famously said, 'You *cannot* be serious!'

Steve Race was at Lincoln School in the 1930s with a boy called Winter Christmas. 'It seemed quite logical at the time,' says Steve, 'and frankly still does.' The one person Steve was most sorry for was the caretaker at Portland Place Methodist Chapel in Lincoln, whose name was Bank Holiday (*FTM*, May 1994). 'I blame the parents', you might say in cases like this – and it certainly behoves those with a potentially embarrassing surname to take great care when naming their offspring, unlike one example I've come across of a Mr and Mrs Pizzie who had a daughter named Lizzie Pizzie.

In August 1994 Lance Wright of Nuthall, Nottinghamshire, told us that he had been collecting unusual first-names from the IGI for people with the surname 'Day'. So far his favourites include Christmas Day, Easter Day, Good Day, May Day and Timeof Day. Maybe somewhere in Australia lurks an individual named G'Day? Almost nothing surprises me any more.

CHAPTER 2

Civil Registration of Births, Marriages and Deaths

From 1st July 1837 all births, marriages and deaths taking place within England and Wales (but not in Scotland or Ireland) were to be officially recorded by the civil authorities, the country being divided into a number of registration districts (each with its own superintendent registrar) and sub-districts for this purpose.

Original records of births and deaths were to be kept at the appropriate superintendent registrar's office, with copies submitted every quarter to a central repository in London. Clergy who conducted marriages in officially-authorised churches or chapels were responsible for submitting quarterly returns to the appropriate superintendent registrar; these were then forwarded to the Registrar General in London. Until the Marriage Act of 1898, marriage ceremonies in non-conformist churches could only take place if the local registrar was present to note the details in his own register; the official record will thus be held by the registrar's office, not in a church register. From 1899 congregations were allowed to keep their own registers and thus dispense with the services of the registrar.

The other alternative for a couple wishing to be married was a visit to the Register Office for a civil wedding, which had to be by notice of marriage or by licence. Since 1995 couples have been allowed to have a civil marriage in an approved building other than a register office.

Researchers interested in obtaining information about a birth, marriage or death which interests them have a number of options:

- Visit, or write to, the appropriate local superintendent registrar, in cases where it is known with some certainty where an event would have been registered. You should be aware that many registration districts have undergone changes over the years, but a telephone call or a letter addressed to the most likely registrar should clarify matters for you.

● Pay a visit to the Family Records Centre at 1 Myddleton Street, Islington, London EC1R 1UW, where national indexes to the centralised birth, marriage and death records since 1837 may be consulted and a certificate ordered. Alternatively, arrange for a friend or a paid researcher to pay such a visit on your behalf. Indexes of civil registration births, marriages and deaths have at last been made available on microform. Purchasing these is an expensive proposition, but sets are held by the Society of Genealogists and at various major reference and local studies libraries.

● Make a postal application by writing to the Postal Application Office, Office for National Statistics, General Register Office, Smedley Hydro, Southport, Merseyside PR8 2HH, giving as many details as possible.

A number of myths and misapprehensions have grown up over the years concerning civil registration of births, marriages and deaths. My paternal grandfather used to believe that his entire family history was available for consultation at Somerset House in London, should he ever wish to pay a visit there to examine it. Years after the indexes of civil

Somerset House: the interior quadrangle. *General Register Office records of birth, marriage and death were held here from 1837 to 1973. (From Thomas Shepherd,* London in the nineteenth century, *1827)*

registration had been moved to St Catherine's House in the Aldwych, people would refer to records being at 'Somerset House', and there are still those who speak of 'St Cath's' long after the move to the Family Records Centre in Myddelton Street.

A particularly charming example of a Civil Registration myth is provided by the well-known *Observer* columnist, Sue Arnold, in her book *A Burmese legacy* (1996). Sue has two British grandfathers and two Burmese grandmothers. Her mother, who is half Burmese, has a strong awareness of race and class, and was particularly keen to find out what she could about her own father, Charles Lloyd:

> *'Promise me you'll find out about Charlie,' my mother says. 'I'd like to know more about him. His cousin, Sir Idris Lloyd, was a big noise in the government you know.' You cannot do better in my mother's eyes than be a big noise. And then she gives me various birth date alternatives – 'It was either 5 September 1865 or 11 November 1856' – which I'm supposed to take round to St Catherine's House. Minutes later (this is what my mother thinks) the attendant comes back and hands me a sheet of vellum printed with a sort of Who's Who entry on the following lines:*
> *LLOYD, Charles Ernest born 5 September 1865 or 11 November 1856, extremely well connected, public school educated, handsome, athletic. Big noise. Married Ma Shweh Ohn with royal connections from Bassein, Union of Burma, one daughter Marjorie, born 1914. Recreation polo. Clubs: Gymkhana, Taunggyi.*

Some hopes!

Don't assume that all civil registration records since 1837 are totally accurate or complete

In theory all English and Welsh births, marriages and deaths since 1837 should be found accurately recorded – which most of them are. For all that, many errors and omissions have been perpetrated, especially in the early years of registration, and it pays to be cautious.

How could errors or omissions have occurred?
1) Non-registration

In the early years, several people viewed the introduction of the registration system with a certain amount of suspicion, and were in no hurry to comply with its regulations if they could avoid doing so.

Until the Births and Deaths Registration Act of 1875, there were no penalties for non-compliance. Not only that, but it was the responsibility of the registrar to search out and to record the fact that a birth or death had taken place; it has been estimated that in some parts of England up to fifteen per cent of births, for example, went unrecorded as a result. In Catholic areas of Liverpool, non-registration of births was as high as 33% in the period 1865 to 1875, and in any case some parents chose to believe that if a child had been baptised, there was no need to register the birth with the civil authorities. The 1875 Act shifted the onus onto the persons concerned to give due notification of a birth or death within specified time limits. There were fines for those who failed to register, or who did so late – that is, more than 42 days after a birth, or more than 14 days after a death. By the same act the guess-work was to be taken out of the registration of cause of death; henceforward an official certificate was to be supplied, signed by a qualified medical practitioner.

2) Inaccurate registration

Even when an event has been registered in the proper way, errors could still very easily have crept in:

- The basic information might have been inaccurately given in the first place. Excited or nervous brides and grooms, proud new parents and recently-bereaved relatives are not always thinking as clearly as they might – and some informants, for reasons of their own, clearly chose to give false details.

- The person writing down the information might have mis-heard or mis-understood what was being said – or might simply have made a mistake in writing it all down.

3) Inaccurate copying

Any situation in which information is copied, by whatever means, leaves the way open for inaccuracies to creep in. Even if a birth, marriage or death was correctly registered in the first place, the copying process which followed might have gone awry:

- The copy submitted to the General Register Office in London by the superintendent registrar or by the officiating minister at a marriage might contain errors – or might not have been sent at all.

- A typescript or handwritten copy certificate provided to a later researcher might be inaccurate.

You might find that parts of a certificate of birth, marriage or death you have ordered are written in manuscript. This could be by way of a facsimile of the original handwriting, or a modern handwritten copy. If

Enter Edward Green. *An interlined entry from the original General Register Office birth index for the March quarter of 1839. Edward Green, born at Stoke on Trent, has been squeezed in between another Edward Green (born in Sheffield) and an Edwin Green (born in West Bromwich).*

the latter is illegible or ambiguous, you'd be justified in claiming that you've paid good money and would like some clarification.

4) Inaccurate indexing

It would be comforting to believe that the index volumes to the centralised records of birth, marriage and death since 1837 were totally accurate. Human beings and human frailties being what they are, however, errors will have crept in. Let's hope it's not you or me who are affected by this!

Early indexes were hand-written on vellum in a flowing copperplate hand, not always so easy to read, despite its careful execution. The good news is that interlined corrections and additions were sometimes made, but the bad news is that some of these were themselves incorrect, or entered in the wrong place – so Rachel Williams in the marriage index for the March quarter of 1856 appears 11 pages away from where she should be.

A suggestion by the Registrar General in 1871 that all the early hand-written indexes should be printed was never taken up at the time. In the event, you will find that the indexes from 1866 to 1910 are printed; those from 1910 to 1970 appear in typescript, and since 1970 they have been printed by computer. It hardly needs to be said that every time an index is converted from one form to another, errors can and do creep in.

In 1970, with the best of intentions, no doubt, the General Register Office began a programme of converting the early manuscript indexes into typescript, thus introducing another stage in the copying process, a further rich opportunity for fresh errors to be made. The typing was not checked; sometimes Roman numerals were incorrectly interpreted, second Christian names were not copied in full, and on occasions complete pages were omitted.

So we pass to a final stage. Eventually the indexes were microfilmed, both by the GRO and by the Genealogical Society of Utah. The GRO films frequently missed pages out, and when in due course the films were converted to fiche, with no quality control in evidence, yet more entries disappeared. No fewer than 600 names were lost as a result of missing pages in the marriage indexes for 1864, and 240 in 1865.

It would be easy to be accused of scare-mongering here, and it wouldn't be fair to exaggerate the situation. Nevertheless, many family historians must have been perplexed at not finding an entry they were confidently expecting to be there, and may, for example, have marked down a family group as being possibly illegitimate because the parents appear never to have married. Details of the sought-after marriage might well lurk somewhere within the General Register Office files, but without an index to assist, any search for it could be doomed to failure.

If the appropriate registration district is known or can be guessed at, examining the superintendent registrar's records of births and deaths may offer the only hope here, and in the case of a marriage, it may be that only the original registers held by the church or chapel concerned will enable you to locate a missing entry.

**Develop strategies for finding entries in the indexes when you aren't successful immediately

It can be bad enough when it's somebody else's fault that you can't find what you are looking for in an index – try not to let it be *your* fault!

- Concentrate and re-visit. It's easy enough to lose concentration when searching many volumes of indexes – especially at the Family Records Centre in London, when someone else might be looking at the volume you need, and you decide to come back to it – but then forget. I'm afraid that your last recourse when all else fails is simply to go through the indexes all over again with your mind even more totally focused on the task in hand – not a happy thought!

- Do check all conceivable surname spellings. You will only have searched the indexes comprehensively once you've checked as many spelling variations for a surname as you can possibly find the time and energy to do. I know this can be a real chore – variants like *Sewel* and *Sewell* should be in the same index volume, though *Lawyer/ Sawyer* or *Milton/Wilton* will not be – but the alternative is that you may not find what you are looking for, when it really is there somewhere!

● Do consider first-name variations in birth, marriage and death indexes. We know that a woman whose birth was registered under the name *Elizabeth* may have been known all her life as *Betty*, or that a man whose official name was *John* always answered to the name of *Jack*. Not only that, but a person may have acquired or dropped a middle name or two as time went by, and the order of his or her first names might have changed. A person you know as Henry George Watson might have been registered under the names of: Henry Watson; George Watson; George Henry Watson, Henry George Charles Watson – or any one of a number of similar varieties.

● Although you might not find a reference you are looking for in the indexes, there may be times when you come up with too many entries for a person with a common name, and can't be sure which is the one you need. Your best bet in such circumstances is to use the Reference Checking system operated by the Family Records Centre. When you fill in a certificate application form, there is space on the back for you to enter further details which you already know; if any of the facts you note in this way do not accord with the certificate applied for, the application will be cancelled and you will be given a part-refund. You can use this service with a Reference Checking Sheet (available from the cashiers) so that checks can be made on a number of possible entries. Be careful when using this checking system: information you have from family sources may itself be incorrect, and you could rob yourself of the chance of obtaining what would have been the correct certificate after all. Consult a copy of the free leaflet, CAS 62, at the Family Records Centre for more details.

● Do think in terms of registration districts, not just in terms of the place where you assume that an event occurred. You might be sure that an ancestor was born, married or died in the Derbyshire town of Ilkeston, for example. Now Ilkeston is a town of substantial size in Derbyshire, but that doesn't prevent it from forming part of the registration district of Basford, which is a much smaller place across the border into Nottinghamshire, but which gave its name to a Poor Law Union upon which civil registration districts were originally based. Some villages – beware! – can lie in more than one registration district, and the districts in question may be in different counties.

Birth

**Expect that there will be some errors or omissions in civil registration of births since 1837

It may be that you cannot find a birth entry in the national or superintendent registrar's indexes. What might be the reason?

- A birth might not have been registered, it might have been registered inaccurately, it might have been copied inaccurately, it might have been indexed inaccurately, or it might not have taken place within England and Wales.

  A bizarre example of a birth never registered at all begins with a boy who was born and baptised Edward, but who died soon afterwards. In the next few years a series of children was born to the same parents until, ten years after the birth and death of the first Edward, the last boy of the family came along and he, too, was given the name Edward. Later in life, the second Edward needed to obtain a copy of his birth certificate, but by this time both parents had died and he had never remembered seeing such a certificate amongst family papers. The appropriate indexes were searched, and he was most puzzled to find there was no mention of his name at the time when there should have been. He later mentioned this to an older member of the family, who informed him that he had had an older brother named Edward who had died; when his parents chose to call him Edward, too, they decided that as they already had one Edward duly recorded, there would be no need to go through the same procedure again and register the boy. After learning of this, Edward went back and promptly found the record of his elder brother and obtained a certificate, using it whenever such a document was required for the rest of his life. Needless to say, he enjoyed a very long and happy retirement!

**Become familiar with the way that birth indexes are organised, and develop ways of finding an entry which eludes you at first

- Can you be sure that a birth took place, or was registered, within England and Wales – not elsewhere in the British Isles, or abroad?

- A birth might have been registered in a district other than the one you were expecting. The parents might have been away from home at the time, or the place of birth – a neighbourhood hospital, perhaps – might not have been situated in the district in which the couple were known to be living at the time. Bear in mind, too, that families living in rented accommodation in urban areas often moved house very frequently.

The Institute of Heraldic and Genealogical Studies has published two coloured maps showing registration and census districts, 1837–1851 and 1852–1946, which show registration district boundaries and will help you make sense of the reference numbers which appear in the 'volume' column of the indexes.

- Still-births and adoptions were only registered in England and Wales from 1st July 1927 onwards.

- Foundlings are located after the letter 'Z' at the end of the national birth indexes for each quarter.

- Some children will be shown in the indexes at the end of each surname spelling simply as 'male' or 'female', with no forename given. This may mean that the parents had not been able to decide upon a name at the time of registration (there being an option for this to be rectified later), or it could be that the child had died before it could be named. You may sometimes find a death certificate but no birth certificate for a child: this will usually mean that he or she died before the birth could be registered.

- During the period 1837 to 1965 about five per cent of births were of illegitimate children. If you cannot find the birth you are seeking in the indexes, it may be that an unmarried mother had given the surname of the father, not her own name, at the time of birth registration – perhaps telling the registrar at the time that she was a married woman.

- If you find yourself working forwards in time – trying to establish the names of children born to a particular couple whose marriage record you already have – then do be open to the possibility that children may have been born earlier than you would have anticipated – either very soon after the marriage, or even before it, to a couple who were not officially husband and wife at the time. A significant number of marriages in England and Wales took place *after* the birth of the first child. Conversely, some couples had children – even the first child – many years after marriage. See under *Marriage*, below.

- Generally never underestimate the ability of some fathers (and some mothers, too) to have children late in life. I have often reflected with some amazement upon the case of Lady Ethelreda Caroline Wickham (née Gordon), the daughter of the Tenth Marquess of Huntly. She was born posthumously in February 1864, and died in

LONG SPAN

Sir—Your correspondents will be unlikely to match the details of Lady Ethelreda Caroline Wickham of Cotterstock Hall, Peterborough, who died as recently as May 9, 1961, aged 97. She was born in February, 1864, the youngest of the 14 children of the 10th Marquess of Huntly— who was born in 1792.

She was almost certainly the last person living whose father was irrefutably born in the 18th century.   Yours faithfully,

D. E. WICKHAM

Belvedere, Kent.

Still alive in the Swingin' Sixties, but with a father born at the time of the French Revolution. *Between them, Lady Wickham and her father had lived through some stirring times* ... [Reproduced with the permission of the *Daily Telegraph*]

May 1961. What is astonishing in this case is that here was a lady alive during the Swingin' Sixties, whose father had been born as long ago as 1792! Meanwhile, in the 'Miscellany' feature of *Family Tree Magazine* (February 1994), Mr K.W. Jones told us that he had spotted an obituary from the *Hampshire Telegraph* of 15th November 1962, which reported the death of Mrs Syndronia Parnell of Southsea, aged 91 years. Her father, Thomas Hobbins, who had served in the Royal Navy in Nelson's day, had been born in 1784, and was aged 87 when he fathered Syndronia. There was life in the old sea dog yet, it seems.

● Also never underestimate the fecundity of some married couples. Owen D. Smithers wrote to *Family Tree Magazine* in June 2000 to tell the tale of a Smithers family not related to him who had brought eight children into the world in just nine years in the 1880s. Eventually, apparently in sheer frustration, they named the last child

'Enough Smithers'. Can you blame them? Researchers using civil registration birth indexes or parish registers of baptism grow accustomed to the fact that a fertile couple will usually be having children every two years or so, based partly upon the mother's lactation cycle. Let this Smithers story give us pause for thought.

● A birth might have been registered later than you would have expected. The Births and Deaths Registration Act of 1875 imposed penalties in cases where a birth was registered more than 42 days after it had taken place. It is not surprising, therefore, that some parents who had delayed taking appropriate action until it was too late were tempted to fabricate a later birth date for their child, rather than have to pay a fine. This may have had the result, of course, of pushing the registered birth into a later quarterly index volume.

Mark Herber tells me that his great grandmother, Bessie Jane Garner, always celebrated her birthday on July 1st, though her birth certificate clearly shows that she was born on 10th October 1881, and that the birth was registered on 19th November following. The July 1st celebrations had remained constant over many years, so it is doubtful that Bessie had simply forgotten when it was that she had been born. A more likely explanation for the discrepancy would seem to be that her parents, Thomas and Ann Garner (née Ship), were keen to avoid paying a fine for late registration in the wake of the 1875 Act, and created a fictitious date of birth for their baby daughter that was forty days before the registration date. In doing so, they seem to have moved as far back towards the genuine July date as seemed prudent. As a result of these shenanigans, Bessie's birth appears in the indexes for the December quarter of 1881, not in the September quarter where you would have expected to find it if you had been told that 1st July was her birth date.

By coincidence (if anything can ever really be a coincidence in family history . . .), a fabricated birth date of 10th October (again) crops up in a tale told to us by Sylvia Durant (*FTM*, April 1994), this time relating to the period before the passing of the Births and Deaths Registration Act of 1875. On this occasion we are looking at a child who was baptised before he was 'officially' born – a great party trick! Sylvia's story concerns the birth and baptism of James Dawes, her husband's great grandfather. His birth certificate was issued on 10th November 1843, giving a birth date of 10th October 1843. But here is the same little James being baptised at Longhope in Gloucestershire on October 8th of the same year!

Malcolm Sutton (*FTM*, July 1994) then told us that his mother had hoped to celebrate her one hundredth birthday on 28th June 1994; the official recognition did not arrive until 4th July, however, since that was the date given by her father when registering her birth. Gwen Rawling had a similar tale to relate, concerning her grandfather; he always celebrated his birthday on 8th August, but discovered that his birth had not been registered until 26th October, giving a false date of birth of 16th September. Both the above discrepancies only came to light, incidentally, when the individuals concerned needed a birth certificate for pension purposes. Gwen's grandfather, meanwhile, forgot to register the birth of one of his own children within the prescribed time, so he picked a date a week or two later. Unfortunately he absent-mindedly chose 29th February – and this wasn't a leap year! The registrar didn't spot the mistake, either.

This was not a unique incident, strange to relate. Daryl Jones sent for a copy birth certificate for his great-great-grandmother's sister, Matilda Birt. The year was 1849 – not a leap year – yet the date of birth was stated to be 29th February (*FTM*, July 2000). I suppose we might even speculate as to whether these unfortunate individuals said to be born on a non-existent day have really ever had a legitimate legal existence at all …

An extreme example of the 'delayed registration' genre came from Mrs Joyce Mellor (*FTM*, July 1994), who sent us a birth certificate for Florence Ethel Dent; this good lady was born on 29th January 1906, but her birth was not registered until thirty years later, in 1936! Joyce guesses that poor Flo probably wanted to get married, and was determined to prove her very existence, original birth registration having somehow slipped through the net.

**Learn how to make sense of a birth certificate and don't be surprised to find that some errors may have crept in

Even if you do find the birth entry in the index and obtain a certificate accordingly, new challenges may well present themselves.

- Details you have taken from parish baptism records may not tally with those given at the time of birth registration. Parents may have had a change of mind between registration and baptism, and the child may have acquired a different set of baptismal forenames than the ones you were expecting.

- Occasionally you will find that a certificate gives no first name for a child. This may be because the parents had not yet decided upon a name (despite having had a fair bit of notice …); it may be that the child's birth and death were being registered at the same time and that no name had been given, or it may be that the child was destined for adoption and that the mother had not wished to give it a name before parting with it.

- If you're really unlucky, you might find that two separate birth dates are given on the certificate. My friend David Herbert of Southwell in Nottinghamshire sent me just such an example recently: Alice Maud, daughter of Frederick Herbert of Willesden, Middlesex, was born on: 'Thirty first of December/10 January 1880', the birth being registered on 17th February following. David's possible explanation for this extraordinary entry are about as desperate and comical as you'd expect in such a situation: 'Long period of labour – head appeared on 31st December 1880 and final delivery on 10th January 1881 … Or maybe the couple couldn't remember the exact date of birth, because they were drunk at the time?'

- Almost any details entered on the certificate might be false, including the gender of the infant. On 22nd June 1912 Reuben Jones was born in the sub-district of Hazel Grove, Cheshire, son of Martha Hannah Ponsonby. So far so good, but an amendment to the original information, made fourteen years later and duly entered by way of a statutory declaration in the right-hand column of a birth certificate issued in 1994, makes a couple of mind-bending corrections. To begin with, the name of the child should have read 'Ruby', not 'Reuben', and furthermore, the child was born a girl, not a boy. I do hope someone told the hapless Ruby that she was a girl after all? (E.C. Jones, *FTM*, July 1994).

Mrs Nellie Pyall sent us a copy of a certificate relating to the birth of Silas Watts, born at Bradwell in Essex in 1873. Nellie reckons that the mother, who registered the birth, may have been so confused and so intimidated by the registrar that she inadvertently gave her own name and sex instead of that of the child! 'Now Mrs. Watts – your name? Louisa. Good. Name of the child? Louisa. Good. Sex of the child? Female. Good.' Not so good – poor Silas's correct details (name, Silas; sex, male) had to be entered in the right-hand column on 9th December 1908 – shortly before Silas emigrated to Canada. Human fallibility and our desire to have historical details accurately recorded don't always seem to be compatible, do they? (*FTM*, October 1994).

- A father's name might mysteriously have become entangled with a description of his occupation. A fine example of this surrealist occurrence on an English birth certificate came from Fiona Knight of Wellington, New Zealand. The birth of Jacob Ludkin was registered on 8th February 1859 at Soham in Cambridgeshire. Name of father: James Ludkin. Name of mother: Mary Ann Ludkin, formerly Talbot. Informant: the father, James Ludkin. Occupation of the father: Farm Ludkin. Try finding that in a dictionary of trades and occupations!

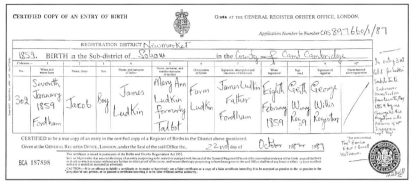

A Farm Ludkin: every farm needs one. *George Willis, registrar for Soham in Cambridgeshire, made an understandable but comical error in January 1859, describing James Ludkin, father of baby Jacob, as a 'Farm Ludkin' rather than a 'Farm Labourer'. Four months later the error was duly corrected and the certificate annotated accordingly.* [Office for National Statistics. © Crown copyright. Reproduced with permission of the Controller of Her Majesty's Stationery Office]

On 14th May 1859 George Willis, the original registrar, made his official note in the right-hand column of the birth certificate to the effect that the father's occupation should read: 'Farm labourer'. I know – you guessed! (*FTM*, October 1994).

- It's easy to assume that if there is a precise time of birth given on a certificate, then the new-born infant must have been a twin, a triplet, or whatever. This is sometimes the case, of course, but in the early years of civil registration a time was often specified even when no multiple birth was involved. You should certainly look out for this happening in the period 1837 to 1839. My namesake, John Titford, was born on 8th September 1839 in Hillwood Lane, Warminster Common, Wiltshire – a single birth; the first column of his birth certificate reads: 'Eighth September 1839; 3 morning'.

- If a birth certificate gives only the name of a mother but no father, it is usually safe to infer that this was an illegitimate birth. Bear in mind, however, that until the Registration Act of 1875, the mother of an illegitimate child was free to name whomever she chose as the father, the registrar having no discretion as to whether he accepted her word or not. After 1875 the father of such a child could only be entered as such if he accompanied the mother and they made a joint registration. If both parents have signed the certificate, then you are safe in assuming that they were not married to each other at the time

– even if their surnames are identical. It would normally be the case that a legitimate child would take the surname of its father; an illegitimate child would take the surname of its mother – and where there is a joint entry, the child could take either name. The Legitimacy Act of 1926 made it possible for a child born out of wedlock to be legitimated by having its birth re-registered if the parents married at a later date. In such cases there will be two separate registrations for the child – the first at the time of birth, and the second once the birth was legitimised retrospectively – often several years later.

● Look closely at column five on a birth certificate, where the mother's name is given. Her maiden name should be given as 'formerly ...', but if she has had one or more previous married surnames, these should be prefixed by 'late ...', if she has volunteered this information.

● The following persons, in order of preference, are currently eligible to act as informants at the time when a birth is registered: the mother; the father (if he is married to the mother); a person present at the birth; the owner or the occupier of a house (or institution); a person who is in charge of the child. Not all such informants, of course, will be able to provide equally accurate information. If the informant at the time of birth registration was not one of the parents, you might have evidence of other family connexions you were previously unaware of.

● If a child is born at some distance from the parents' usual address, then they have had the option since 1875 of attending their own local registrar to have the birth registered. In such cases the details are posted to the registrar where the birth took place, and the certificate will bear the words: 'By declaration dated ...'.

● It is extremely rare to find any extraneous or uncalled-for information entered on a birth certificate, but you might come across the occasional exception, as Ronald J. Linford did in 1994, prompting him to write to Jean Cole's 'Questions and Answers' feature in *Family Tree Magazine* for November of that year. Ronald's late sister-in-law, Mary Stringer (née Blackwell) was born on 6th September 1909 at Sheringham, Norfolk, a sub-district of Erpingham. The following text was added to her birth certificate by the registrar:

Presented free to Miss Mary Blackwell, being a copy of the first entry made in the parish of Sheringham, since the formation of the new Sheringham sub-district.

This was a generous gesture, to be sure, providing one of the few examples we are ever likely to see of an 'add-on' comment on a formal birth certificate.

● In July 1969 birth certificates were redesigned so that the old familiar 'landscape' format (that is, with the long edge at top and bottom) was replaced by a 'portrait' style (short edge at top and bottom), the overall size being altered to metric A4. The full address of the father, mother and informant was added, as was the place of birth of both parents. From April 1995 the mother's occupation is also given.

Before we leave the subject of births, a passing but chilling thought might not come amiss. Mrs J. Crowley of Llanbadarn Fawr, Dyfed, tells us that an elderly friend once told her that her grandmother, a midwife, used to consider it acceptable to exchange a much-wanted but still-born baby for a healthy baby born to an unwilling mother. Now have nightmares about that one! (*FTM*, August 1994).

Marriage

**Expect that there will be some errors or omissions in civil registration of marriages since 1837

The process whereby marriages were registered with the civil authorities from 1837 differs significantly from that which applies to births and deaths.

At a Church of England wedding, the relevant information is written out three times: once on a certificate which is handed to the happy couple (at my own wedding the best man promptly gave this to my wife, and I've never seen it since!); once in a register which is retained by the church, and once more in another register which is kept until it is full (though this may take several years) and then submitted to the superintendent registrar of the appropriate district. Not only that, but every three months the minister must also prepare further copies of all the marriages that have taken place during the previous quarter; these are submitted to the appropriate superintendent registrar, who forwards them to the Registrar General in London. They will eventually be included in the consolidated national index for that quarter.

A helpful printed guide for the use of clergy, entitled *Suggestions for the guidance of the Clergy relative to the duties imposed upon them by the Marriage and Registration Acts*, published in 1904, defines this copying process in the following terms (the eccentric use of capital letters at the start of some, but not all, nouns, has been retained):

> ... The Rector, Vicar or Curate of every Church and

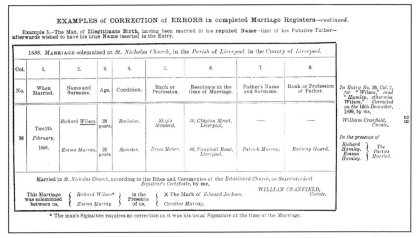

Registering marriages was a complex business. *A sample certificate included in an appendix to* Suggestions for the guidance of the Clergy relative to the duties imposed upon them by the Marriage and Registration Acts, *published by the Registrar General in 1904, which informs clergy what to do if an illegitimate man has used the name of his putative father at the time of marriage, but then wishes his real name to be registered after all.*

Chapel, shall, in the months of April, July, October and January respectively, make and deliver to the Superintendent Registrar of the District in which such Church or Chapel may be situate, for transmission to the Registrar-General, a true Copy, certified by him under his hand, of all the Entries of Marriages made in his Registers during the previous Quarter ... The Copies must be made on unmutilated leaves of the Forms supplied by the Registrar-General for the purpose ... The Copies must be literal transcripts of the Entries in the Register Book, reproducing even the inaccuracies which occur in the originals. If any name appears to have been misspelt in the Register Book, it must be spelt in the same way in the Copy ... Signatures need not be imitated, but should be legibly written ... The delivery of Quarterly Certified Copies to the Superintendent Registrar is usually made through the Registrars of Births and Deaths in his District ... For delivering a true copy of every Marriage Entry, duly certified, the Superintendent Registrar shall pay or cause to be paid to the Rector, Vicar or Curate, the sum of Sixpence for every entry contained in such Certified Copies ...

A clergyman by the name of Rev. Allan Newman Guest had a nasty shock on the morning of 20th March 1909, when the postman delivered a letter to him from Somerset House. He had only recently been appointed to the living of Stantonbury with New Bradwell, near Stony Stratford in Buckinghamshire, but was very soon informed by the authorities that one of the churches for which he was responsible, St James New Bradwell, had never been formally licensed as one in which marriages could be solemnized. Not only were there intending brides and grooms waiting to be married there in the near future, but no fewer than 434 couples had stood at the altar of St James since 1860, only to discover in retrospect that their marriage was invalid, and that their children were consequently illegitimate. It took an Act of Parliament to sort out this very unpleasant anomaly eventually, but not before a lot of people had lost a fair amount of sleep as a result of it (details from an article by Alan Dell, *FTM*, August 2000).

A similar system to that which applied to Anglican churches was used *mutatis mutandis* for registering details of marriages which took place in Register Offices, or those conducted in the presence of a civil registrar (or, after 1898, an authorised person under the terms of the Marriage Acts) in buildings used for Roman Catholic or non-conformist worship and duly registered for the celebration of marriages. Jews and Quakers, who had earlier been excluded from the stipulations of Lord Hardwicke's Marriage Act of 1753, were legally entitled to conduct their own ceremonies after 1837, but had to submit full details of their marriages every quarter to the Registrar General.

I once had cause to refer to a marriage certificate for a Jewish family I was working on for a client. Jonas Ellis married Sarah Jacobs on 30th March 1840, according to the rites and ceremonies of the New Synagogue of German and Polish Jews, 'Marriage solemnized at 28 Petticoat Square in the Union of East London in the County of Middlesex'. The address seemed familiar, but it wasn't until a while afterwards that I realised that the couple had been married, not at a synagogue, but at the home of the bridegroom's parents, Lambert and Sarah Ellis – a not uncommon practice at the time (see *The story of the Ellis Family 1655–1999* by Susan Bronkhorst, 1999, pp.60–62). The fact is that a synagogue does not have to be a special building – it is simply defined as a place where four male Jews meet together.

All this adds up to a fairly complex bureaucratic process – and complex processes, we know, are very prone to errors being made. It was a bold and optimistic move in 1837, to hope and expect that 15,000 clergy throughout the country would willingly co-operate with a civil system of registration which some found distasteful or unnecessary, and all would find something of a chore. The hapless clergyman who failed to sit down once a quarter and make retrospective copies of marriages

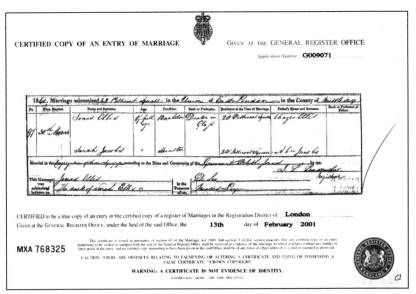

Married at home in 1840. *Jonas Ellis married Sarah Jacobs according to the rites and ceremonies of the New Synagogue of German and Polish Jews at 28 Petticoat Square, London – the home of the bridegroom's parents. Nothing has been entered in the 'rank or profession' column for either of the two fathers.* [Office for National Statistics. © Crown copyright. Reproduced with permission of the Controller of Her Majesty's Stationery Office]

entries for the benefit of the General Register Office in London would be fined £10. Many must have tackled the task with a sorry grace, despite the modest fee they received – little wonder, then, that much of the handwriting gave evidence of being hurried and slapdash. For all that, their submitted registers were never checked – a recipe for disaster in some cases.

In principle, registration of marriages should be complete since 1837. That this is far from the case was graphically illustrated in 1999 by the publication of *'A comedy of errors' or the marriage records of England and Wales 1837–1899* by Michael Whitfield Foster of New Zealand, the result of six years' work during which no fewer than 300,000 entries were examined. 'Comedy' is one way of putting it; what is revealed in Foster's book is more akin to tragedy, describing, as it does, a situation which is enough to make you weep. The author came to the conclusion that, at its worst, there could be many as a million entries missing from the indexes to marriages in England and Wales between 1837 and 1899.

An article based upon Foster's book by Anthony Camp, former

MARRIAGE FORM.

To be sent to the Verger or to one of the Clergy before the
Marriage Service

Full Christian Name and Surname (Male)

Geoffrey Richard Walshe

Age.... *29*

Bachelor ~~or Widower~~

Occupation

Residence at time of Marriage

Christleton , " Lamorna "

Father's Full Christian Name and Surname

Occupation of Father

Date and Hour of Marriage *1 June .*

Banns 7 May 16. 21.

Full Christian Name and Surname (Female)

Lillian Mary Moore

Age *25*

Spinster ~~or Widow~~

Occupation

Residence at time of Marriage

Worthenbury, Flint

Father's Full Christian Name and Surname

Herbert Moore &c

Occupation of Father *Local Registrar .*

2/6 paid

Church Monthly Office, 33, Craven Street, Strand, W.C.2

The Comedy of Errors could begin here. *Rev. A.A. Guest Williams, rector of Christleton, Cheshire (from 1926), would arrange for couples intending to marry to fill in their details on a form printed for that purpose by the Church Monthly Office. The completed form would be returned to the rector himself or to the verger, presumably in order that marriage certificates might be prepared in advance of the ceremony. The handwriting here is not the most legible we will ever see, and could be subject to misreadings, though the bride's father was a 'Local registrar'. Could this give rise to a series of copying errors of the kind which beset so much marriage registration?*

Director of the Society of Genealogists, appeared in *Family Tree Magazine* for March 1999, and usefully summarises the book's findings, some of which will be incorporated as we proceed with this sorry saga. Michael Foster didn't rest on his laurels once his book had been published: in October 1999 a number of further discoveries he had made were featured on the Internet as part of Fawne Stratford-Devai's 'English and Welsh roots' column in *The Global Gazette (Canada's Family History Magazine)*. This may be found at: http://globalgazette.net/gazfd/gazfd38.htm

Here again the fundamental point is stressed that, given the errors that have crept in over the years and the problems of identifying the correct marriage for a person with a common surname, '... the only valid basis for the records lies with the original registers. Going back to those records would make it possible to create new and effective indexes with even more identifying features'.

For all that, it is usually advisable to use the national civil registration indexes to locate a marriage, since superintendent registrars' records of marriage will be incomplete for some parishes, and may well not be organised in such a way as to permit ease of reference.

In earlier and inexperienced days, my wife and I once tried to obtain a certificate for the marriage of her great-great grandfather, Thomas

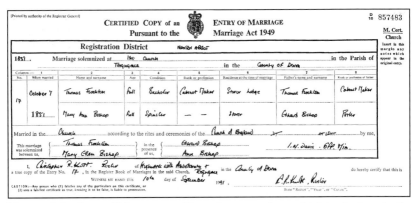

Not much business. *This copy certificate for a marriage which took place in the small Devon settlement of Teigngrace in 1851 was written out by the local rector in 1991, at which time the original register book issued in 1837 was still in use. Note that the bride, who signs as 'Mary Ellen Bishop', has been incorrectly entered (on the original certificate, presumably) as 'Mary Ann Bishop'. Such inconsistencies are commonplace.* [Office for National Statistics. © Crown Copyright. Reproduced with permission of the Controller of Her Majesty's Stationery Office]

Flockton. Although he had been born in Huddersfield in Yorkshire, we knew that Thomas had married in the remote Devonshire parish of Teigngrace, near Newton Abbot. A letter to the superintendent registrar at Newton Abbot elicited a reply in the shape of a typescript form, stating: 'The register with that particular entry is still in the hands of the incumbent ...'. The address of the incumbent in question was added in manuscript, along with the helpful comment: 'Teigngrace parish church still has its register from 1837!' A marriage register has space for 500 entries, and there had clearly been fewer than that number of marriages in Teigngrace since 1837. In the event we did get a certificate from the incumbent (Thomas's wife being given as 'Mary Ann Bishop', but signing as 'Mary Ellen Bishop' – par for the course, we thought ...), but the lesson was clear: the registrar couldn't make out a certificate from a register which hadn't yet been filled and so had never been deposited with his office. This cannot be a unique instance.

**It may be that you cannot find a marriage entry in the national indexes. What might be the reason?

- A marriage might not have been registered, it might have been registered inaccurately, it might have been copied inaccurately, or it might have been indexed inaccurately.

- A number of clergy could not remember when the quarter days fell throughout the year, despite reminders being issued. In the summer of 1840 marriage returns for St James church in Bristol were submitted eighteen months late. Others which arrived late were never indexed at all – so of three entries of marriage for Childerditch ranging in date from May 1842 to July 1843, submitted in November 1845, only the first is indexed. Entries which arrived early may also never have found their way properly into the system, and you could search for them in the indexes in vain.

**Become familiar with the way that marriage indexes are organised, and develop ways of finding an entry which eludes you at first

- Can you be sure that a marriage took place within England and Wales – not elsewhere in the British Isles, or abroad?

  Even when a marriage has been duly registered in England and Wales, there are reasons why you might fail to find or to recognise it in the indexes. It's almost a case here of trying to imagine what sort of errors could creep in, and then expecting the worst. Sometimes the father's name was indexed instead of that of the groom; one party to the wedding might be indexed, but not the other; sometimes the sex of one of the parties might be changed, *Hannah* White appearing as *Henry* White; entries on the back of a page might be missed and not indexed; even fairly legible writing might be mis-read, giving *Tench* in place of *French*.

• The marriage might have been registered in a district other than the one you were expecting. The general principle was that a couple would marry in the bride's parish, but this rule was not universally adhered to. As a variant on this theme, Michael Whitfield Foster was surprised to find no marriage entries at all for the district of Shrewsbury in his computer listings for 1881 and 1891, and the local Superintendent Registrar can only suggest that they might have been filed by the General Register Office with those for nearby Atcham.

• If you are unable to locate a marriage using a woman's known maiden name, do consider the possibility that she had previously been married, but then widowed or divorced, and that her married surname, not her maiden name, will appear in the marriage indexes. A woman may have been married and widowed more than once, of course; in such a case she should be using the surname of her last husband, but there is always the potential for errors or misunder-standings to occur in such situations.

• The marriage you are seeking might have taken place later than you were expecting – either just before the birth of the couple's first child (in the first half of the 19th century, almost one third of all brides were pregnant), or even years later, after many or all of their children had been born. Alternatively, of course, a couple may never have married at all. Consider the possibility that in the years before divorce was affordable, one or both partners may have had a spouse who was still alive and living elsewhere. Bigamous marriages, of course, were not unknown in such circumstances.

• A marriage might have taken place much earlier than expected. I once obtained a birth certificate for a client which showed that his ancestor Richard Sayers was born on 16th December 1897 in Tunstall, Staffordshire, son of Joseph Sayers and his wife Elizabeth (née Talbot). Adopting the usual practice, I worked backwards in time looking for the marriage which had led to this birth. It's lucky I was patient: Joseph Sayers had married Elizabeth Talbot in Goldenhill, Staffordshire, on 1st August 1869 – over 28 years before their son Richard's birth! This would seem to give a whole new meaning to the term 'extended family'? I would never pretend that this was a normal state of affairs – but the principle that you should sometimes expect the unexpected is graphically in evidence here.

● If you had details of the birth of a couple's first-born infant, how long before that birth would you look in order to find the relevant marriage? In my own case you'd have to look back 15 years – that's how long it took my unfortunate but patient parents to welcome me into the world. If we step outside the realms of civil registration for a moment, however, it's worth remarking upon a memorial inscription at St Michael, Highgate, North London, which declares that John Smith (buried 31st March 1790) had only been born following 'the prayers which his most religious mother daily offered at the throne of grace for the space of 30 years altogether, during which time she had been childless ...' (Grace Cowie, *FTM*, August 2000). If would-be parents can be so patient, we might say, then so should we be as researchers ...

● If looking for a marriage of a person whose birth you already know, don't assume that all brides and grooms were in the flush of youth. Widows, widowers, or divorcees who remarried could be getting on in life, and it's certainly not unknown for there to be a great discrepancy in the ages of a couple at the time of marriage – the groom usually, but not always, being older than his bride. Children may follow! Not only that, but many people choose to enter into matrimony when they are well into middle age; in my immediate family, for men and women to get married for the first time over the age of 50 is almost the rule, rather than the exception.

● If you're looking for a remarriage of a person recently widowed, do start the search very soon after the death of the first spouse. A poor widow or widower could not afford to be too sentimental and to settle down to an extended period of grieving before looking for a new husband or wife, especially if there were children to care for, and the workhouse loomed.

● You might not have found evidence of your great grandfather's wife's demise in the death registers, yet here he is in the marriage indexes, taking on a new wife. You could somehow have missed the relevant entry of death, or it might have gone missing, but there is a very real possibility here that the second marriage was a bigamous one – not such a very uncommon occurrence in the days before divorce was readily available, though many couples chose to live together rather than commit bigamy.

Double or multiple entries in the indexes

If you fail to find a marriage in the indexes and suffer a fit of depression as a consequence, you may feel little enough sympathy for those who encounter the opposite problem. On occasions there will be a case of *embarras de richesse* where the same marriage has been indexed more than once.

It is not unknown for an absent-minded clergyman to have submitted details of the same marriage more than once. Not only that, but in cases where the clerical handwriting was difficult if not impossible to decipher, the clerks at the General Register Office would often include variant spellings in the index. So it is that you will find an entry for Kington, Shropshire (page 723, volume 6a) in 1881 listed separately under *Henry Coombes, Henry Coomby* and *Henry Coventry*. One person, three index entries. Luckily, for the year 1881 at least, these conflicting spellings can be compared with the census return for that year in an attempt to arrive at some kind of definitive spelling of the surname.

If a man known as Thomas Henry Smith signed the register simply as 'Thomas Smith', both variants would be indexed. Registers were usually completed as far as possible before the ceremony – indeed, they still are – but at the time of the wedding itself, Peter Shore might sign as Peter Shaw, or Mary Smith as Mary Smyth. At least two entries in the subsequent indexes are better than none, you might say, though you might become confused when using an index made out in this way.

Occasionally – very occasionally – you might find that a couple married not once, but twice. Sometimes a bride and groom went through the formalities at a Register Office and then chose to undergo a church ceremony as well. The Registrar General made a valiant attempt to insist that in such cases no official record of the second ceremony should be made. His exhortations sometimes went unheeded, alas, and you will occasionally come across the kind of double-entries that he was so keen to avoid.

In December 1993 Barbara Samples wrote to *Family Tree Magazine* with copies of two marriage certificates. Redmond Clements MacDowell, bachelor, married Sophronia Elly Combs, spinster, at St Marylebone Parish Church in London on 4th April 1859. But just a minute: here is the same Redmond Clements MacDowell, still describing himself as a bachelor, marrying the same Sophronia Elly Combs, still a spinster, at St Luke's, West Holloway, on 29th December 1863. Both marriages were by licence, and the parentage given is the same in both cases. Here's another example of our old friend, belt and braces ...

Do persevere in your use of civil registration marriage indexes. Only when you have looked high and low should you assume that the marriage might never have taken place, that a clerical error has hidden it from view – or that it took place outside England and Wales. When using the early indexes it is always good practice to locate the names of both the bride and the groom, making sure that they bear identical reference numbers and that the year and the quarter tally, before ordering a certificate. This is normally a foolproof method, but be aware that each page of a marriage register, bearing its own reference number, will contain not one, but two, marriage entries. There is still a slim chance that you might order an incorrect certificate as a consequence, especially if the surnames involved are common ones. After March 1912 things get a little easier, as the surname of the spouse appears alongside each main index entry.

**Learn how to make sense of a marriage certificate and don't be surprised to find that some errors may have crept in

Even if you do manage to negotiate all the pitfalls and obtain a certificate for a marriage which interests you, more challenges of interpretation might lie ahead of you and more errors might be encountered.

- Any of the details given on the certificate could contain errors. This can be worrying enough if such a mistake is obvious, but more worrying still if all seems in order and you only unearth the inaccuracy later – or not at all.

  The married couple might have got their facts wrong, been misheard or misinterpreted. The person officiating might have made an initial error or a copying error, and any later copy might not be a true duplicate of the original.

  Mark Herber, in his book *Ancestral Trails* (1997), tells the story of how he and a cousin both ordered the same marriage certificate, only to find that the address, *Mundford* Road, was accurately transcribed on the one, but falsely given as *Standford* Road on the other.

  George Fitch came across a marriage certificate in which the male surname is spelt in three different ways. The groom is a *Fitch*; he signs as *Ffitch* and a witness appears as *ffitch*. There is no reason to suppose that a copying error was being perpetrated here, and bearers of this surname must get used to the odd spot of confusion; George himself became simply 'Fitch' because the double-letter feature was becoming too much of a nuisance. The double 'f' at the beginning of the name is simply an old way of representing a capital letter 'F', and therefore should, in all conscience, be spelt using two lower-case 'f's. To use the form 'Ff' is simply doing the capitalization job twice over!

- One or both parties might have signed with a cross (x). What conclusions can you draw from this? Bear in mind at this stage that the copy certificate issued to you, unlike the original marriage register, does not include the actual signatures of any of the parties, and that you have thereby lost any possible clues to identity that a signature might have offered. There is a chance, of course, that the original register was signed with a name, not a cross, though this is an unlikely eventuality. A person using a cross as an identifying mark might well have been illiterate, as a third of men and a half of women appear to have been during the early years of registration, and if this were the case, of course, they would not be able to check the accuracy of the information written in the marriage register. Remember, however, that a bride or groom making a cross might have chosen not to sign, rather than have been unable to. Many a bride would not wish to upstage her illiterate new husband by signing her name when he could not, and there was a general feeling around that it would be unlucky if she were to do so. Also consider the possibility that a person who signed a marriage register confidently enough might have learned to perform this particular trick, but yet have been unable to write anything else besides.

- The couple getting married may both have given the same address for registration purposes. What might be the significance of this – had they been 'living tally' as they say in some parts of the country? Not necessarily so. Given the fact that the church required at least one of the parties to have been resident in the parish for a minimum of four weeks before the marriage, and that two sets of banns would have had to be paid for if the man and the woman admitted to living in different parishes, it is hardly surprising that many used the same address – or neighbouring houses – as an 'accommodation address'.

- It should be clear from a marriage certificate whether the bride was a spinster, a widow or a divorcee, this being stated in the fourth column. A woman would be married under her last married name, not her maiden name, though, if necessary, the latter can usually be inferred from her father's name, if given.

- Always look carefully at the names of witnesses; these may be strangers, roped in on the day, but more usually they will be friends or relations. You may have evidence here of family connexions you didn't previously know about.

- Can you always trust the bride and groom's ages as given on a marriage certificate? No. A person described as being 'of full age' could be anything over 21, no matter how old, and '21' itself could mean the same thing. A 'minor' would be below the age of 18 after 1969, below 21 before that, but as young as 14 (boys) or 12 (girls) before 1929. So far so good, but it was quite possible for one or both parties to lie about their ages, or simply to have forgotten (or never to have known) how old they were. If one or both parties were minors, they may have boosted their ages in order to marry without parents' consent, and if an older woman was marrying a younger man, she might have decreased her age and/or he might have increased his, in order to avoid any mockery – even in the days before the term 'toy boy' had been invented.

• Can you always trust the accuracy of the father's name as given by each party to a wedding? Absolutely not. A number of shadowy characters, including step-fathers, might find themselves featured in the 'father' column on a certificate. Equally, there may be no name given at all if illegitimacy was involved or if the father's name was simply unknown.

It was only after a good few months of frustrated searching and thinking that I eventually realised that 17-year-old Jane Best Titford, who married a bricklayer named Charles Skevington at St Pancras Old Church, London, on 26th July 1857, was not, as she claimed, the *daughter* of 'James Titford, deceased', but the *grand-daughter* of the said James – who was then very much alive, thank you very much. The truth was that Jane Best was the illegitimate daughter of Mary Ann Titford (born in 1816 in Wylye, Wiltshire, daughter of James); presumably Jane's father's surname was 'Best', and she had acquired both names.

Generally, don't place too much faith in the presence or absence of the word 'deceased' after a father's name. In the above example, father (well, grandfather, as it happens ...) was still alive, yet is said to be dead; you will find other instances in which father was deceased, but where the fact is not noted.

Giving Grandad's name as father's name at time of marriage was not an uncommon occurrence, as it happens, and many a girl must have thought that naming a genuine member of the family, though not the right one, would take the edge off her white lie. After all, what was a poor girl to do? Admit to all and sundry on her wedding day that her father – even if she knew his name – had never been married to her mother? No, better to fabricate a father for the day.

The subject of fabricated fathers exercised the minds of a number of readers of *Family Tree Magazine* during 1992, and many wrote in with stories of their own. Mrs Denise Skeates sent in copies of two marriage certificates: one for Frederick Albert Elms ('Father: Frederick Albert Elms: doubtful if correct name') and another for Frederick Albert's sister, Eliza Elms ('Father: Illegitimate child of Jane Elms'). You either fabricate, then, or you tell the truth bluntly as it is. And if you do fabricate, you can always invent a totally non-existent person if the mood takes you. Sheila Holley had to come to

Fabricated fathers. *In 1857 a bricklayer named Charles Skevington married Jane Best Titford at St Pancras Old Church (shown here as it was in 1820). Jane provided the information, which was duly recorded, that she was the daughter of 'James Titford, deceased'. Not so. She was the illegitimate daughter of Mary Ann Titford, and James Titford (not at all deceased at the time) was her* grandfather. *(From Walford's* Old and New London)

the conclusion, eventually and reluctantly, that the 'Edward Fenn, coachman', named by her grandfather as his father when he married, was simply a figment of Grandad's imagination. Fiona MacNaught had come across two marriage certificate oddities: one bride named her elder brother as her father, and another claimed that her father was dead – when in fact he was alive and well and living with a woman other than his legal wife (*FTM*, June 1992). One last bizarre example came from Barbara Samples (*FTM*, November 1992), whose great grandfather, Thomas Patrick Augustus McCann, chose for some odd reason to give his mother's maiden name (MacMahon) as his own surname at the time of his marriage. Name of father? Well, it was really John McCann, but Thomas, unorthodox to the last, named him as 'Charles MacMahon'. Whatever can have possessed him?

The good news when it comes to illegitimacy and marriage, of course, is that a birth certificate for an illegitimate child may give only the name of the mother, but when the child grows up and is to be married, he or she might know father's name and provide it at the time of registration (A good point made by Mrs R. A. Harlow, *FTM*, November 1992).

- Bear in mind, finally, that some marriages could last a mighty long time. In 1997 and 1998 readers of *Family Tree Magazine* wrote in with examples of couples staying together for periods in excess of 70 years. The record had to go to the grandparents of Richard Coomber: Rowland Pearson and Frances Isabel Butcher. They married at Hartfield in Sussex during September 1912, and their marriage lasted until Rowland died in January 1990, by which time they had spent over 77 years together. As it happens, Rowland was a leap-year baby, born on 29th February 1892, so had had only 24 'real' birthdays. Just think, married for 77 years and still only aged 24 ...

Death

**Expect that there will be some errors or omissions in civil registration of deaths since 1837

From 1837 onwards, burial (or cremation) was only permitted on the production of a death (or coroner's) certificate, so in theory death registration should be fairly complete. However, it may be that you cannot find a death entry in the national or superintendent registrar's indexes. What might be the reason?

- A death might not have been registered, it might have been registered inaccurately, it might have been copied inaccurately, it might have been indexed inaccurately, or it might not have taken place within England and Wales.

  An unusual example of an entry in the death indexes which could scupper your research completely was sent to *Family Tree Magazine* in August 1992 by Rhoda Windiate-Blackmore. In this case a man's army rank of Major has been shown as his first Christian name, and his second initial has been entered incorrectly. It would be a brave and bold family historian who was prepared to look in the indexes under 'C', for example, in the hope of finding Colonel John Brown there ...

**Become familiar with the way that death indexes are organised, and develop ways of finding an entry which eludes you at first

- Can you be sure that a death took place, or was registered, within

35

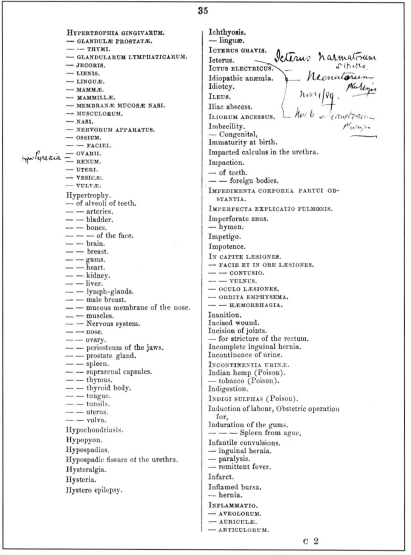

HYPERTROPHIA GINGIVARUM.
— GLANDULÆ PROSTATÆ.
— ·— THYMI.
— GLANDULARUM LYMPHATICARUM.
— JECORIS.
— LIENIS.
— LINGUÆ.
— MAMMÆ.
— MAMMILLÆ.
— MEMBRANÆ MUCOSÆ NASI.
—· MUSCULORUM.
— NASI.
— NERVORUM APPARATUS.
— OSSIUM.
— — FACIEI.
— OVARII.
— RENUM.
— UTERI.
— VESICÆ.
— VULVÆ.
Hypertrophy.
— of alveoli of teeth.
— — arteries.
— — bladder.
— — bones.
— — — of the face.
— — brain.
— — breast.
— — gums.
— — heart.
— — kidney.
— — liver.
— — lymph-glands.
— — male breast.
— — mucous membrane of the nose.
— — muscles.
— — Nervous system.
— — nose.
— — ovary.
— — periosteum of the jaws.
— — prostate gland.
— — spleen.
— — suprarenal capsules.
— — thymus.
— — thyroid body.
— — tongue.
— — tonsils.
— — uterus.
— — vulva.
Hypochondriasis.
Hypopyon.
Hypospadias.
Hypospadic fissure of the urethra.
Hysteralgia.
Hysteria.
Hystero epilepsy.

Ichthyosis.
— linguæ.
ICTERUS GRAVIS.
Icterus.
ICTUS ELECTRICUS.
Idiopathic anæmia.
Idiotcy.
ILEUS.
Iliac abscess.
ILIORUM ABCESSUS.
Imbecility.
— Congenital,
Immaturity at birth.
Impacted calculus in the urethra.
Impaction.
— of teeth.
— — foreign bodies.
IMPEDIMENTA CORPOREA PARTUI OBSTANTIA.
IMPERFECTA EXPLICATIO PULMONIS.
Imperforate anus.
— hymen.
Impetigo.
Impotence.
IN CAPITE LÆSIONES.
— FACIE ET IN ORE LÆSIONES.
— — CONTUSIO.
— — VULNUS.
— OCULO LÆSIONES.
— ORBITA EMPHYSEMA.
— — HÆMORRHAGIA.
Inanition.
Incised wound.
Incision of joints.
— for stricture of the rectum.
Incomplete inguinal hernia.
Incontinence of urine.
INCONTINENTIA URINÆ.
Indian hemp (Poison).
— tobacco (Poison).
Indigestion.
INDIGI SULPHAS (Poison).
Induction of labour, Obstetric operation for,
Induration of the gums.
— — — Spleen from ague.
Infantile convulsions.
— inguinal hernia.
— paralysis.
— remittent fever.
Infarct.
Inflamed bursa.
— hernia.
INFLAMMATIO.
— AVEOLORUM.
— AURICULÆ.
— ARTICULORUM.

c 2

Registering deaths was a complex business. *In 1886 the Registrar-General published an* Alphabetical list of diseases and causes of death *for the use of registrars of death, being a reprint of the second edition of an* Index to the nomenclature of diseases *drawn up by the Royal College of Physicians. The owner of this particular copy of the list has made a few additions of his own in manuscript.*

England and Wales – not elsewhere in the British Isles, or abroad?

● A death might well have been registered in a district other than the one you were expecting. If Uncle Percy was on holiday in Skegness when the reaper called, his death will be registered there, not back in Nottingham where he lived and worked – unless his body were brought home for burial. When Brenda Norbury Harrison and her father went to register her mother's death, the registrar asked for the place of birth of the deceased. 'Nightingale Lane, Hornsey,' said father. 'Derby,' said Brenda, well-versed in the family's history. Father was desperately upset by the death, naturally enough, so the registrar settled for 'Hornsey'. Here's an inaccuracy in the making, though it was allowed to happen for the most humane of reasons (*FTM*, June 1993).

● You can usually expect that a death will be registered very shortly after it has taken place, but the need to carry out an inquest could have caused a delay, even one lasting several months. Keep searching the indexes further forward in time, just in case.

● Indexes after March 1866 give the age of the deceased at death, and from June 1969 his or her date and place of birth are provided. In theory this can be a great help, but do remember that it will have been an informant who gave this information, not the poor speechless deceased person him or her self. To quote a telling phrase used by Anthony Camp in one of his lectures, 'Dead people cannot state their ages'. Neither a grieving relative nor a stranger present at the death might have had any accurate idea as to the person's age or date of birth – especially if the deceased person had been lying about his or her true age for years previously.

● It is worth noting that an entry which gives the age at death simply as 'O' will relate to the death of an infant, someone who did not live out a full year.

● The last death index volume for each quarter is used to register unidentified bodies, with an estimated age added. Generally, and for obvious reasons, this is of little help to family historians.

**Learn how to make sense of a death certificate and don't be surprised to find that some errors may have crept in

Even when you have obtained a certificate for a death which is relevant to your research, more challenges of interpretation might lie ahead of you and more errors might be encountered.

- Age at death might be inaccurate – see above.

- If there have been errors made in the death certificate, and if you're lucky, officially-sanctioned corrections will have been entered in the far right-hand column. A certificate for 'Minnie Shaine' had had to be amended in this way in nearly every respect: her name was really Welhelmina Scheu, her age had been entered inaccurately, and 'Parentage unknown' had originally been entered in the 'Occupation' column (Norma Rawlings, *FTM*, August 1993).

- In theory no additional information should appear on a death certificate any more than on a birth or marriage certificate, but the eminent Jewish family historian, Dr Anthony Joseph, once came across a case in which the words 'His father died of the same complaint aged fifty four' are written beneath the cause of death (*FTM*, May 1993).

An even more unusual – and libellous – interpolation was brought to our attention by Winifred Waterall from Loscoe in Derbyshire (*FTM*, October 1994). John Massey, a 72 year old farmer from Repton, was murdered in May, 1910. His death certificate is bold or foolhardy enough to name the supposed murderers:

Cause of death: fractured skull caused by blows on the head with a blunt instrument inflicted by Amos Peel and John Dugan.

Now this certificate was issued even before the murder trial had begun – a trial at which both Peel and Dugan were acquitted from lack of evidence! What price *sub judice*?

- Don't be too concerned if the occupation of the deceased isn't what you were expecting (the same applies, of course, to birth and marriage certificates). Many people had a number of ways of earning a living during their lifetime or followed more than one occupation simultaneously, and sometimes the same job could be described using different terms. Remember again that it was an informant who gave this information; he or she might simply have been making a guess, or have preferred one occupational title to another.

When James Titford (born at Wylye, Wiltshire, in 1780) was admitted to St Pancras Workhouse, London, in September 1861, he gave his occupation as 'Catsmeat dealer'. This was, indeed, one of the ways he had earned his living, though he had also been an agricultural labourer, a french polisher, a chapel keeper and a general meat salesman.

'Only a *sixth* class funeral, Sir? Only *one* horse?' *William Titford's father, a former agricultural labourer and catsmeat salesman, died in St Pancras Workhouse in 1862. Nothing daunted, a year later 'W. Titford', fashionable undertaker, was charging his wealthier clients the princely sum of £29 for a first-class send-off. (Advertisement from a London Directory of 1863)*

His children aspired to greater social status than he had ever enjoyed, however, and his son William was rapidly making a name for himself as a fashionable North London undertaker. So when old James died in the workhouse at four o'clock in the morning of 15th June 1862, said to be aged 84 (he was actually 82), the authorities were informed by his next-of-kin that he had been a 'Clothes salesman'. This was very probably a fib, but at least it freed the deceased from any final association with cat's meat. Similarly, a very distant cousin of James the Catsmeat, my own great-great grandfather Benjamin Titford (1814–1879), who was originally apprenticed to a silversmith, still used this fairly genteel term to describe his occupation, even though he had since been a pawnbroker's assistant, a lodging house keeper and a humble clerk.

Married women were not shown as having an occupation in their own right on death certificates until 1969; previously they would simply be described as 'Wife/widow of John Smith' or some such – which in itself could be a valuable piece of information to family history researchers. A deceased child would be described (until 1969) as 'Son/daughter of John Smith, carpenter', no mother's name being stated except in cases of illegitimacy.

● The stated cause of death (be it uncertified, certified by a medical practitioner, certified by a post-mortem but with no inquest, or certified after an inquest) could be accurate, or it could be a guess. In

Disarmingly honest. *It was 'probably apoplexy' which carried off Jesse Keane at the age of 48. Not all registrations are quite so honest about any doubts concerning the cause of death.* [Office for National Statistics. © Crown Copyright. Reproduced with permission of the Controller of Her Majesty's Stationery Office]

the early years, most deaths were uncertified, but after 1875 the cause of death is usually followed by the words: 'Certified by ... [James Gordon MRCS LRCP]'. A certificate issued in respect of Jesse Keene, a 48 year old gamekeeper from Lindfield in Sussex, who died on 19th April 1883, gave the cause of death as *'probably* apoplexy'. Few death registrations were quite as disarmingly honest as this one; in most cases of uncertainty, we may suppose that one possible cause of death was chosen and entered accordingly, without any doubt being expressed.

● Words written in the 'Cause of death' column may be unintelligible to a layman. Having struggled to make sense of some obscure-looking medical terms on one such certificate, I sought help in printed books. First I turned to a slim volume: *Alphabetical list of diseases and causes of death [reprinted for the use of Registrars of Deaths from the second edition of the Nomenclature of Diseases drawn up by the Royal College of Physicians of London]* (1886). Once I knew from referring to this simple list of illnesses what the words on the certificate *could* read, I came up with 'Albuminuria' and 'Anasarca'. Not much the wiser, I then made use of a later edition of the same work with the title *The nomenclature of diseases, drawn up by a joint committee appointed by the Royal College of Physicians in London,* 6th.Edition (1931). Here there was an attempt to classify each affliction, so 'Albuminuria' turned out to be a urinary disorder, and 'Anasarca' was yoked together with dropsy as a 'disease of the areolar tissue'. Finally I made use of one of those wonderful little volumes that used to sit on all our bookshelves a few years ago, *Collins family medical encyclopedia* (1952). Now all became clear. 'Albuminuria: ... Albumen is present in the urine ... may constitute an important sign of disease ... likely to arise in kidney disease ...'; 'Anasarca: Generalised dropsy ... abnormal accumulation of fluid in the body tissues and cavities ... results mainly from kidney and heart disease ...'.

● A person described as being 'in attendance', and who might well have provided information to the registrar, may not have been present at the time of death, but simply caring for the deceased during his or her last days. In any case, think carefully about the identity of the informant who reported the death; this person's relationship to the deceased is usually stated, and it might be a relation of whose existence you were previously unaware.

● Do try to make further investigations if a death certificate indicates that an inquest was held. See *Coroners' records in England and Wales* by J. Gibson and C. Rogers (2nd edition, 1997) for more details.

● In July 1969 death certificates were redesigned, becoming A4 'portrait' in format, and the usual address of the deceased person was provided in addition to details of the place at which he or she died.

In case we might believe that errors on death certificates are restricted to England and Wales, let's finish with a couple of examples from the United States of America. Commander David Lund had a real problem interpreting the death certificate of his great-great uncle, who died in Minnesota. If you were to accept the certificate at face value, then the deceased was born on 30th [sic] February 1868, was buried on 5th December 1908 (three days before he died), and had his death certificate filed eleven months before the date of death (*FTM*, July 1995). I suppose this shouldn't surprise me – a Californian death certificate dated 10th October 1924 for my first cousin (twice removed), Marwood James Henry Titford, not only omits his first name and refers to him as *Harvey* in place of *Henry*, but also gives his father's name as 'Curry Rivel Titford' (he was born in Curry Rivel, Somerset). Better than Tandoori Masala Titford, I guess?

There are several published books which deal with civil registration records. In particular you are recommended to read *The Family Tree Detective* by Colin Rogers (Manchester University Press, 3rd edition, 1997), a trouble-shooting guide to civil registration and much else: *People count: a history of the General Register Office* by Muriel Nissel

(HMSO [OPCS], 1987); and Tom Wood's *An introduction to civil registration* (Federation of Family History Societies, 1994) and two companion volumes by Barbara Dixon: *Birth and Death Certificates, England and Wales 1837 to 1969* (1999) and *Marriage and Certificates in England and Wales* (2000).

CHAPTER 3

Census Returns

Census returns for England and Wales from 1841 onwards include the names of individuals, but there is more to be gleaned from them than purely genealogical information. Our motive for consulting these wide-ranging records may be to determine relationships within a family and the age and birth place of our ancestors, but we would do well to linger on an entry that interests us, not simply to scoop up what seems most relevant and then pass on to something else. A close look at the street or area in which those ancestors were living can help to build a broader picture of their world, and censuses have always been a happy hunting ground for those who like an insight into human oddities, frailties and peccadilloes. A census return, after all, is very often the nearest we will get to a 'fly on the wall' insight into the lifestyles of our Victorian ancestors.

Few census returns yield up all their riches at a first glance, and we need to develop strategies both for finding a relevant entry in the first place, and then for making full sense of it once it has been found.

**Don't be surprised if you can't find some people where you expected them to be in the census

Most family historians, thank goodness, find most individuals they are looking for on the census most of the time. All will have stories of disappointment to tell, however, and certain of our ancestors seem at times to have hidden themselves from view quite deliberately. If you can't find a person or a family you are looking for in the census, what might be the reason?

Missing completely

● It may be that the enumerator simply missed a particular family, a

Grosvenor Square: censusless in 1851. *By some bewildering oversight, Grosvenor Square in London was apparently missed out of the 1851 census completely. (From Walford's* Old and New London*)*

house or even a whole area completely when doing the rounds. It could not have been difficult in overcrowded towns or cities to overlook the occasional house or tenement, though more worrying is the fact that Grosvenor Square in London was apparently missed out completely in 1851. This was a rare occurrence, luckily, though some returns have inexplicably gone missing, including those for the Kensington, Paddington, Golden Lane and Whitecross sub-districts of London (1841) and for the Belgravia and Woolwich Arsenal sub-districts (1861). As if that were not bad enough, the 1851 returns covering Salford and parts of Manchester have suffered severe water-damage; such information as can still be extracted from these documents is currently being extracted and published by the Manchester and Lancashire Family History Society.

Susan Lumas in her book *Making use of the census* (1992) recounts some harrowing tales of missing census entries:

> *An enumerator in Manchester has explained the lack of information for one particular address by 'gross carelessness on the part of the Lodging Housekeeper. When I informed*

More pressing priorities than providing information to the census enumerator.
This family group of 'Manchester operatives', living in Southern Street, Liverpool Road, in 1862, may well have had better things to do with their time than help a census enumerator complete his returns accurately. (From the Illustrated London News, *29 November 1862*)

> *him to read the Schedule and told him of the penalty, it was all to no purpose, he said he asked their names and they would not tell him' (RG 10/4051, f.160, p.51).*
>
> *In another case an enumerator has explained, 'consequent upon a general row when tables were turned over, three forms were destroyed and the names of thirty-seven persons, all males, of ages varying from 19 to 60, were lost' (RG 11/322, f.35, p.16).*
>
> *'John Travers will not give any information respecting the persons who abode in his house on the night of June 6th only that the number was 125'. There is a note by the registrar that 'Mr Travers [was] fined £5 at the Mansion House by Sir Peter Lawrie June 23rd 1841'. (HO 107/732, book 12, f.6, p.6).*

● Censuses were not popular with the population at large; some regarded them as an unwarranted invasion of privacy, while others saw them as a devious method of compiling listings which would be

Mr Turner is not at home. *It is said that the artist, J.M.W. Turner, was canny (or paranoid) enough to have spent the night on board a ship moored in the Thames in order to avoid the census man's visit. (From Walford's* Old and New London*)*

used for tax purposes or as a means of detecting people who should be sent back to their parish of settlement under the stipulations of the Poor Law.

J.M.W. Turner, the painter, is said to have spent the night on board a boat moored in the Thames in order to avoid the census snoopers, and criminals and others may well have had a vested interest in lying low. Few opponents took such extreme measures as Agnes Strickland, author of *The lives of the Queens of England*, however. In 1871 she and her sister, opposed to the census on principle, spent the night driving around the lanes in a hired cab, safe from the reaches of the enumerator for Southwold, Suffolk. As far as we know, he never caught up with them (Richard Howard Johns, *FTM*, April 1993).

● There are certain groups of people who were simply not recorded in some of the earlier censuses. In 1841, for example, no returns were made for members of the Royal Navy on board ship, members of the merchant marine, fishermen at sea or the crews of vessels engaged in inland navigation. Also in 1841, itinerants, travellers or night-workers were not included, and a fair number of these seem to have been missed off later censuses, too.

Not where you would have expected

The person you are looking for may have been recorded in the census, but not at the address you were expecting.

● Families living in urban areas often moved house frequently, especially if they lived in rented or leased accommodation. Others did a 'moonlit flit' in order to escape creditors or the rent man.

● Urban street names were often changed, as were the house numbers within each street. In 1908 my paternal grandfather managed to secure a mortgage allowing him to pay the £320 necessary to take out a 99-year lease on a newly-built house in Bowes Road, New Southgate, London. The house was numbered 225 when he bought it, but it wasn't very long before it was renumbered as 231. On occasions, even more confusingly, two houses would bear the same number, at least for a while.

House numbers are often not listed on a census return, and it is not normal to find them at all in the returns for 1841, where what may appear to be a house number entered in the extreme left-hand column is simply a schedule number.

You should search an entire street for an individual or a family you are seeking, then. Do be sure that you have checked every house, bearing in mind the fact that the enumerator would proceed down a main thoroughfare until he came to a side-street, which he would then tackle before returning to his original route. This can get very complicated in some towns and cities.

Even then you could miss a house or a person. Colin Rogers, in *The Family Tree Detective* (3rd edition, 1997), tells of Arthur Harry Pole, who was born at 4 Mycock Street, Manchester, in May 1862. At the time of the 1861 census the street had not been built, but by the 1871 census its name had been changed. Meanwhile, Mr B. Chambers (*FTM*, April 1993) has a recurring nightmare that if a person was born just after one census, and if his birth was not registered for some reason, and if he then died at the age of nine, he could have lived 'nine years of his life for nothing'. A far-fetched case, but I see what he means.

Two examples of census returns from America can serve to provide an interesting contrast to areas of densely-packed population in Britain where it is hard to find a person you are looking for. One return for McCulloch County, Texas, for 1860 reveals no inhabitants whatever, while the enumerator for Wichita County, Kansas, came across a place which was home to five buffalo hunters, four bone-pickers, three mustang catchers and a cowboy. He managed to elicit the names of ten of these local worthies, but noted that the rest 'positively refused to answer any questions and I considered it safest to not press any inquiries' (Nicholas Newton-Irving, *Genealogists' Magazine*, March 1997, page 374).

● A person you are seeking may have been absent from home on census night for reasons of his or her own: working away from home, visiting friends or relations, on holiday, in hospital, in the armed forces ... A 'stray' entry sent to the Derbyshire Ancestral Research Group in 1994 solved the mystery of a man missing from home on the 1881 census for Ripley, Derbyshire. Far from his home town, he was serving a five year sentence in Pentonville Prison, London, having been convicted for night poaching and assault at Derby Assizes in 1877. The 1881 Pentonville census only just caught our friend – he was released in July of that year – and this story bears out the fact that a person can get up to an awful lot of capers between censuses, returning to the fold in time for census night as if nothing had ever happened (Winifred Waterall, *FTM*, April 1994). If you are looking for a seafaring or boat-loving ancestor, you will find listings of ships on rivers or within territorial waters at the end of the appropriate districts; after 1861 some, but not all, ships on the high seas or in ports abroad were enumerated in a separate schedule at the end of the main returns. The Public Record Office holds an alphabetical list of names of ships taken from these schedules, and an index on microfiche to those people who were on board ship in 1861 (only) has been compiled by the Genealogical Society of Utah.

• If you have found a reference to an ancestor in a surname or street index, you will probably have a folio number to work on. Do remember, then, that each folio number covers two pages; you should look at the page which bears the folio number, but also the *next* page, which will be the 'verso' or reverse side of the sheet.

• There were those who believed, or chose to believe, that a very young baby – especially one that hadn't been baptised or given a name yet – need not be included in a census return, not yet being a 'real person', as it were.

• Then there were those people who were said to be present at a given address on census night but weren't really at home at all. It was acceptable practice to include those who were working on night shift as if they were present at the home they would return to in the morning, but some heads of household clearly chose to list members of their family who would usually live at the house but were temporarily absent. In such cases individuals could be listed twice: at their usual home address and also at the place where they actually spent census night.

Not bearing the name you would have expected

All the usual warnings about taking a flexible approach to first names and surnames apply to census as to other records. It's worth knowing that in 1841 only one forename was to be given; in 1851 the enumerator was told that the initial of a second Christian name '*may* be inserted', and this became '*must* be inserted' in 1891. Generally be cautious about every name you find, and don't despair too soon about those you cannot find. Most names will be rendered accurately, but opportunities for mistakes to occur were legion.

**Do think carefully about relationships as stated on the census

Relationships are not stated on an 1841 census return, and have to be inferred – though you should do so with care, given the scant amount of information at your disposal. From 1851 the concept of a Head of Family was introduced, each individual then being defined in terms of his or her relationship to this person. The so-called Head was deemed to be primarily responsible for a family, though may not have been the oldest person within the group. Sometimes a widowed mother might be defined as the Head, while in other cases her son or daughter might have taken over as the principal breadwinner, leaving widowed Mum to be defined as 'Mother' of the new Head.

Do exercise great caution when it comes to the defined relationship between other family members and the Head. A 'brother-in-law' might be a step-brother; a 'daughter' might be a daughter-in-law; a person defined as the 'child' of the Head might really be a grandchild, the son or daughter of a married couple who are also listed within the family group. The term 'nurse child' might refer to a boy or girl who had been adopted, but it could simply be applied to a child who was staying overnight.

The terms 'boarder' and 'lodger' could be confused and confusing, and a person described as a 'visitor' might turn out to be a relation after all. Someone who is said to be a 'servant' might not have been employed by the family in whose house he or she was living at the time of the census, and in any case a so-called 'servant' or 'housekeeper' might have had a more intimate relationship with an employer than the term would seem to imply.

**Don't always trust the accuracy of information as it appears on a census return

There are many reasons why information which appears on a census return may not be accurate or comprehensive. Some people knowingly gave false information – because they objected to the census in principle, because they were afraid that it would lead to their being taxed, or because they thought that it would be great fun to have some nonsense about them recorded for posterity. Others would simply have been unsure about the facts they were asked to provide, so an age, birthplace or exact relationship to the head of the household may have been guessed at.

Whether the information provided was accurate or not at the outset, there were plenty of opportunities for error. Did the enumerator hear, understand and correctly write down that which he was being told? Was his handwriting legible? Was the information then copied accurately later, and was anything lost or distorted when the manuscript returns were microfilmed?

It has always seemed to me a case of Sod's Law that whenever I refer to a census on microfilm, I whizz past pages of wonderfully clear writing, only to find that the entry I need is in the semi-invisible section, looking as if someone has tried to rub it out with an eraser.

Why might information be inaccurate?

Those who objected to the census may not have hired a cab in order to be away all night, as in the case of the two good ladies quoted above, but may have shown their displeasure by giving false information to the enumerator, as in the case reported in the *Hull Advertiser* on 18 June 1841 (Joyce Mumby, *FTM*, November 1993):

> *Summonses were granted at Marylebone Police office last week against two ladies for refusing to give correct returns. One of them was an elderly lady, occupying a portion of some premises who, instead of filling up the page properly, had, at the bottom of the column in which her age should have been inserted, drawn with a pencil a human head and written against it the word 'Guess'.*

Two more naughty ladies!

Even those who had no intention of hoodwinking the enumerator may have done so inadvertently. Not a few hapless souls when asked to state their age and their place of birth seem to have gone into a flat spin or to have had a nasty attack of amnesia. This is perhaps no great surprise: we all have to take such facts on someone else's say-so, since we may have been around at the time, but were too young to make sense of anything very much.

Remember that on the 1841 census, ages for individuals older than fifteen were usually rounded down to the nearest five. Other than that, a person of either sex might have chosen to claim that they were younger than they really were for reasons of vanity, and an older person might have chosen to glorify his or her status by adding a year or two, as old folk still do today when they proudly announce that they are in their 'eighty-fifth year'. Isabella Bownass, christened 'Bella' and born in Seathwaite, Lancs, had the endearing habit of telling every census enumerator that she was the same age as her husband, when in fact she was four years older (E. Jean Dunn, *FTM*, August 1992). I'm reminded of the apocryphal story of the Mullah who was asked how old he was. 'Forty five,' was the reply. 'But Mullah, I asked you the same question four years ago, and you gave me the same answer.' 'Yes, I know – that's because I always like to be consistent in what I say ...' Something similar may possibly have happened occasionally at census time?

Under the Factory Acts children were not allowed to work until they had reached the age of 13, so it must have been a significant temptation for parents whose offspring were flouting the law to have added the odd year or two for census purposes. Servants, on the other hand, might have inflated their stated age in order to qualify for higher wages.

Defining a place of birth wasn't always as easy as it might seem. As a child I lived in a place called Woodside Park, North London. Really it felt as though we were in Finchley, though we paid rates to Hendon, were a few yards from the border with Hertfordshire but actually within Middlesex, undeniably in London, and would eventually form part of the London Borough of Barnet. Place of birth? Well now, let me think ...

Variation in the spelling of place-names was common enough generally, but particularly so in Cornwall and in Wales, and a Welsh birthplace given in an abbreviated form as 'Llanfair', for example, might refer to a multitude of places, as Edward Higgs explains in *Making sense of the census* (1989). If you possibly can, do check and compare birthplaces given by your ancestors in more than one census. One of the most effective ways of identifying a very obscure place in England and Wales is to refer to one of the indexes of place-names published at the time of the census from 1831 onwards. Look for separate index volumes published for the 1921 and then the 1951 census onwards; thousands of places, from cities to tiny 'localities' are mentioned, making these books some of the most detailed gazetteers you could ever hope to use.

It's bad enough, you may say, that a person wasn't sure where he or she was born, or couldn't decide exactly how to define the place. Much worse if the same person gave a different birth-place on successive censuses! Let me share with you a few examples of this unfortunate and not uncommon practice, taken from the pages of *Family Tree Magazine* for August 1992.

Jane Stubbs from Eastbourne has an ancestor who was born in Barton, Bedfordshire – or in Pulloxhill, or Shillington, take your pick. To make matters worse, the lady in question couldn't decide whether her name was Charlotte Paper or Mary Papworth. Then there is Elizabeth Goulding, née Stone, who was baptised in Crich, Derbyshire, of parents from nearby Tansley. As we proceed from the census return for 1851 to that of 1871, she gives her place of birth as Derby, then Tansley, then Elton. It could have been worse: these are neighbouring yet distinctively different places, but at least all are within the same county (Ian Goulding). Much more surrealist is the case of the great-great-great grandfather of Neil Fox of Tettenhall. Place of birth from the census? Shifnal, Shropshire; Long Kantrell, Herefordshire; Holly Green, Radnorshire; Presteigne, Radnorshire; Witton, Radnorshire. What a jolly jape, then, to dream up a new birthplace every ten years – especially since 'Long Kantrell, Herefordshire' and 'Holly Green, Radnorshire', appear not even to exist!

Elizabeth Ebben, née Prime, told the 1851 enumerator that she came from Ingatestone, Essex (where her husband was born), but in 1861 she chose Enfield, Middlesex, the birthplace of her children. Of course she came from neither place: in 1871 she chose Sawbridgeworth, Herts, and, wonder of wonders, this was correct (Celia Jepps).

And where was William Roads born? Banstead, Surrey? Wotton, Surrey? 'On the Sea' – or Gibraltar? Gibraltar! Oh, yes, the place of that name just outside Epsom, of course (Mr K.R. Rhoades).

So do be flexible in your thinking. 'Oh, no,' you may say, 'my George Smith was the one who was 45 years old, not 47, and he was born in Wymondham, not Norwich.' We seek perfection, consistency, and we get upset when we don't find it. Do allow for the possibility that your ancestors – or those who gave information on their behalf – might have made mistakes.

Finally, of course, we should expect that errors may have crept in as the enumerator attempted to make some sense of what he was being told, especially if the informant had a strong dialect or poor diction. Alan Turner (*FTM*, October 1992) points out very pertinently that birthplace – and other – errors in this field are more likely to occur when the terms 'ditto' or 'do' have been used without due care.

**Expect to find some anonymous individuals on the census

It was common practice to give initials rather than full names for those unfortunate individuals who found themselves living in certain institutions such as workhouses or lunatic asylums at the time of the census. You might be able to work out the identity of 'J.B. Patient. Married. Aged 47. Female. Needle worker', though it could demand some careful thought. Workhouses, hospitals, prisons, asylums and military barracks were given the status of enumeration districts in their own right, providing they accommodated at least 200 people. You will find them at the end of each district, on a special form with no address column.

A variation on this theme may be found in the 1891 census for the Lincolnshire County Asylum. Two of the entries read: 'Unknown Man 1' and 'Unknown Man 2'. Mr I.G. Morris, who sent a copy of this entry to *Family Tree Magazine* in June 1994, found it rather bewildering: all right, so these unknown men may not have been *compos mentis* enough to give their names – but then how did the enumerator know that one was a 22 year old married shoemaker born in Ireland, and the other a 29 year old married blacksmith born in Lincoln? Very odd. Another enumerator could come up with the names of lunatics all right; it was their place of birth that caused him a headache: 'The omission of the place of birth in the case of the Lunatics are too frequent; but I was utterly at a loss to make them out from their incoherency' (RG 9/647, f.87, p.39. Quoted in *Making use of the census* by Susan Lumas).

It wasn't only paupers and lunatics who might be anonymous or semi-anonymous, however. A young baby not yet named, if he or she was included in the census at all, might simply be referred to as 'infant' or some such. When the census man visited my great grandparents Alfred and Mary Buckler at 17 Lockhurst Street, Hackney, in 1881, they needed to include their one-week old daughter, as yet un-named. She was described in the returns, rather charmingly, as 'Baby Buckler'. Meanwhile, south of the Thames in the same year, the Lovelock family at 56 Bermondsey Street, Bermondsey, had recently taken delivery of a baby son a mere two hours before midnight. In the 'occupation' column is written: 'Baby born 10 o'clock – night of third'.

Readers of *Family Tree Magazine* in mid 1992 had great fun trying to find the youngest child ever recorded in a census. Mrs Shirley Morris told us that her grand-daughter Alexandra Tyson was born at 11 pm on Sunday, 5th April 1981, so was only one hour old when she was entered on the census for Beckenham Maternity Hospital (*FTM*, June 1992); an 1841 entry for Radcliffe-on-Trent, Nottinghamshire, features George Widdowson, aged 5 minutes (Bryan Bailey, *FTM*, June 1992); and in Melksham, Wiltshire (1881) the un-named and un-christened daughter of Emma Deverall had been born at 11.57 pm – so we are down to a child aged a mere three minutes (*FTM*, August 1992). Is that as young as we can get? Not a bit of it! Trevor Harris from Perth, Western Australia, had been computerising the 1841 census returns for England; after only a six-minute search of 750,000 records in his database, he came up with the last word on the subject. Down in Berkshire no age is entered against 'Infant Daniels', but in the 'occupation' column there is an annotation which reads: 'Infant born at 12 o'clock'. This certainly seems to refer to midnight, not noon, and gives us an age of – well, zero, I guess? (October 1992). There, naturally enough, correspondence on this subject came to an end.

Expect the census to reveal great mobility in certain families

Family historians are often warned not to believe the charming myth that families stayed in one town or village for generations, rooted to the spot. If the surname you are researching is a rare one, you can often use a variety of records to track a family as it moves from place to place, but in most cases it is the census above all which provides incontrovertible evidence of mobility and of migration.

Particular groups of people were more mobile than others, as Stuart Folds from Orpington found when he located an ancestor who was a hawker of hardware in the 1861 census. The man himself had been born in Glasgow in 1811; his wife came from Portsmouth, and their children were born in Brecon (Wales), Alloa (Clackmannanshire, Scotland), Wrekenton (Durham) and Duns (Berwickshire, Scotland). Without the help of the census, this might almost have been a case of 'My ancestor is untraceable ...' (*FTM*, March 1992).

When canals were first being built, they would often be referred to as 'navigations', and consequently the itinerant workers who built them were known as 'navigators' or 'navvies' for short. As time went by, navvies were employed in the building of railways or roads, and the very nature of their work meant that they rarely stayed in one place for very long. Anne Mills wrote to *Family Tree Magazine* in June 1994 to tell us of a family group she found in the 1891 census for Chesham Bois. This village doesn't have its own station, but tracks to the nearby towns of Amersham and Chesham were being built at this time. So we have William Sampson, born in Devon, and his wife Sarah, from Cardigan. Each of their children was born in a different county – Sarah in Staffordshire, George in Sussex, Arthur in Surrey and William in Buckinghamshire. Nice if you want to know where the family had been living, but horrible if you once lose them!

**Learn how to get the best out of the 1881 census on CD-ROM

Few developments in the world of family history in recent years have been greeted with so much joy – and relief – as the publication of the 1881 British census on CD-ROM. Following years of dedicated effort by volunteers, whose work was co-ordinated by the Federation of Family History Societies and processed thanks to the computer skills and software made available by the Church of Jesus Christ of Latter-day Saints (LDS), the final product was made available on microfiche, and eventually by way of 24 CD-ROM disks.

Family and local historians have been having a field-day ever since, locating individuals they thought they would never find, searching up and down neighbouring streets, trawling through occupations and birthplaces. Not only that, but it's amazing what you can stumble across by accident – or serendipity.

One person I was looking for lived in Newington in Surrey, at an address referred to as 'Messrs Tarns Establishment'. Contemporary commercial directories revealed that William Tarn & Co were 'Linen drapers, silk mercers, boys' & ladies' outfitters, boot makers, carpet warehouseman, ironmongers, bedding, bedstead & general cabinet furniture manufacturers' of 165 to 173 Newington Causeway SE – a kind of Department Store by any other name. Clearly they employed a significant number of staff, and it looks as if they housed many of them in a kind of huge dormitory or hostel of their own. 'Messrs Tarns Establishment' was headed by Joseph Haines, a house steward, supported by three housekeepers, three porters and 20 domestic servants. These good people lived on the premises and catered to the needs of a very large number of Tarn employees: 34 drapers' clerks, 10 milliners, 3 dressmakers and 148 draper's assistants – a total of no fewer than 222 persons, all bachelors and spinsters except for Elizabeth Allen, assistant housekeeper, who was a widow. Such a place, a mixture of unmarried males and females mainly in their teens, twenties or thirties, must have taken some policing!

Other oddities of various kinds have come to light. James and Elizabeth Criddle and their six children, aged between seven and twenty-five years, appear no fewer than four times on different returns in the village of North Petherton, Somerset (RG11/2372 folio 11, page 16; 2373 folio 61, page 16; 2375 folio 114, page 39 and 2375 folio 117, page 45). There are only very minor discrepancies between these entries and it is clear that all of them refer to the same brickyard labourer and his household (Mrs Maureen Criddle, *FTM*, January 2000). A word of possible explanation for this disturbing duplication was offered to *Family Tree Magazine* in August 2000 by Doreen Brown, who had been a rural census enumerator herself, and so understood the way things worked. It seems that enumerators were only given a map, without addresses, and in some cases a house within a village could be situated at the meeting point of four enumeration districts and so be inadvertently included four times.

Without being ungrateful for all the work done on their behalf by an army of unpaid volunteers, a number of users of the census on CD-ROM have reported inaccuracies they have uncovered in the course of their researches. For such a project to be error-free would, of course, be an unexpected miracle. I quickly stumbled across a transcription mistake myself. Great grandparents of mine by the name of Robert and Mary Archibald were listed with four of their children. The middle name of my grandmother Margaret and of her brother James, which should have read 'Willox' was given as 'Wilcox', though a look at the original return soon revealed that this was an understandable error made by the enumerator himself. More bizarre, however, was the fact that the person transcribing for the microfiche and CD-ROM versions had represented *Ringcroft* Street, Islington, as *Kingcroft* Street. Reference to any London street atlas would have avoided such a slip. I don't complain – this kind of minor lapse is as nothing compared to the glorious luxury of having this census transcription made available – and at such a bargain price!

A different kind of error can occur if the first-named person in a household is entered singly at the bottom of one page; occasionally he or she is listed as a separate household from the rest of the family, who appear on the next page or pages.

Each researcher will have his or her own favourite tricks for getting the best out of the information stored on the CD-ROM disks. You can now buy modestly-priced computer programs which enable you to

1881 British Census

Name		Status	Age	Sex	Place
John A. BICKLE		U	20	M	Week St Mary, Cornwall, England
	Occ: Drapers Clerk				
Frank BIRD		U	17	M	Clifton Bristol, Gloucester, England
	Occ: Drapers Clerk				
William J. BULL		U	21	M	Camberwell, Surrey, England
	Occ: Drapers Clerk				
Samuel W. COAD		U	19	M	Stepney, Middlesex, England
	Occ: Drapers Clerk				
Samuel B. COCHRANE		U	17	M	Clapham, Surrey, England
	Occ: Drapers Clerk				
Ernest E. COLLARD		U	16	M	Gravesend, Kent, England
	Occ: Drapers Clerk				
Joseph COLTMAN		U	21	M	London St Margarets & St Johns , London, Middlesex, England
	Occ: Drapers Clerk				
Arthur CREASY		U	19	M	Streatham, Surrey, England
	Occ: Drapers Clerk				
John H. CUMINGS		U	15	M	Chelsea, Middlesex, England
	Occ: Drapers Clerk				
Frederick T. C. DAVIS		U	15	M	St Georges Southwark, Surrey, England
	Occ: Drapers Clerk				
John H. DENMAN		U	18	M	Islington, Middlesex, England
	Occ: Drapers Clerk				
Percy DRISKELL		U	17	M	Camberwell, Surrey, England
	Occ: Drapers Clerk				
John HARE		U	32	M	Freston, Suffolk, England
	Occ: Drapers Clerk				
Charles P. HOLLOWAY		U	15	M	Portsmouth, Hampshire, England
	Occ: Drapers Clerk				
John HORSBURGH		U	23	M	Smethwick, Stafford, England
	Occ: Drapers Clerk				
William ISBISTER		U	27	M	Stenness Kirkwall, Orkney, Scotland
	Occ: Drapers Clerk				
George Wm. LAW		U	14	M	Ealing, Middlesex, England
	Occ: Drapers Clerk				
Frederick S. MAWSER		U	24	M	Camberwell, Surrey, England
	Occ: Drapers Clerk				
Gilbert W. PALMER		U	15	M	Islington, Middlesex, England
	Occ: Drapers Clerk				
Alfred R. PARSONS		U	16	M	New Romney, Kent, England
	Occ: Drapers Clerk				
Arthur PEARSON		U	17	M	Maidstone, Kent, England
	Occ: Drapers Clerk				
Godfrey A. PUGH		U	15	M	Brixton, Surrey, England
	Occ: Drapers Clerk				
Samuel P. RENTELL		W	40	M	Linton, Cambridge, England
	Occ: Drapers Clerk				
Samuel B. RINGER		U	25	M	Fressingfield, Suffolk, England
	Occ: Drapers Clerk				
Alfred De Lacy ROBINSON		U	16	M	Kepple Street W C, Middlesex, England
	Occ: Drapers Clerk				
Edward W. SHEARING		U	17	M	Ellingham, Norfolk, England
	Occ: Drapers Clerk				
William R. SMITH		U	15	M	Ashtead Nr Epsom, Surrey, England
	Occ: Drapers Clerk				
Arthur E. TAYLOR		U	21	M	Camberwell, Surrey, England
	Occ: Drapers Clerk				
William A.P. TIDDY		U	15	M	Pimlico, Middlesex, England
	Occ: Drapers Clerk				

An employees' dormitory. *William Tarn & Co had a large drapery business in Newington Causeway in south-east London, and accommodated nearly 200 of their unmarried staff in their own large dormitory. Some of the drapers' clerks featured in the 1881 census listing of Tarn employees are shown here. (From the 1881 Census on CD-ROM, a joint venture by the Church of Jesus Christ of Latter-day Saints and the Federation of Family History Societies)* [PRO RG11/0534. Reprinted by permission. Public Record Office. Copyright © 1998, by Intellectual Reserve, Inc.]

1881 British Census

Dwelling:
Census Place: North Petherton, Somerset, England
Source: FHL Film 1341571   PRO Ref RG11   Piece 2372   Folio 11   Page 16

	Marr	Age	Sex	Birthplace
James CRIDDLE	**M**	**45**	**M**	**Taunton, Somerset, England**

Rel: Head
Occ: Brickyard Labourer

Dwelling:
Census Place: North Petherton, Somerset, England
Source: FHL Film 1341571   PRO Ref RG11   Piece 2373   Folio 61   Page 16

	Marr	Age	Sex	Birthplace
James CRIDDLE	**M**	**45**	**M**	**Taunton, Somerset, England**

Rel: Head
Occ: Brickyard Laborer

Dwelling: North Petherton
Census Place: Bridgewater, Somerset, England
Source: FHL Film 1341571   PRO Ref RG11   Piece 2375   Folio 114   Page 39

	Marr	Age	Sex	Birthplace
James CRIDDLE	**M**	**45**	**M**	**Taunton, Somerset, England**

Rel: Head
Occ: Brickyard Laborer

Dwelling: North Petherton
Census Place: North Petherton, Somerset, England
Source: FHL Film 1341571   PRO Ref RG11   Piece 2375   Folio 117   Page 45

	Marr	Age	Sex	Birthplace
James CRIDDLE	**M**	**45**	**M**	**Taunton, Somerset, England**

Rel: Head
Occ: Brickyard Laborer

Entered four times in the 1881 census. *The 1881 census lists the family of James Criddle, bricklayer of North Petherton in Somerset, no fewer than four times. The returns are practically identical, but each has its own separate piece, folio and page number within class RG11. (From the 1881 Census on CD-ROM, a joint venture by the Church of Jesus Christ of Latter-day Saints and the Federation of Family History Societies)* [Reprinted by permission. Public Record Office. Copyright © 1998, by Intellectual Reserve, Inc.]

navigate your way through the data in a more effective way, and Version 3 of the Resource File Viewer, issued by the LDS Church, allows you to search for a specific word or words – including an address or occupation.

One piece of advice I would offer is to think laterally – that is, in particular, to look for the neighbours if you can't immediately find the individuals you seek. To while away the odd hour or two, I had spent some time transcribing an original manuscript autobiography of a non-conformist minister by the name of Josiah Bull, born in 1808 in Newport

Pagnell, Buckinghamshire. His account of his life makes it clear that he was living in Burns Street, Nottingham, in 1881, and I thought it would be fun to find him in the census. Going straight to the 'Midlands East' computer disk, I typed in his name. No success. I decided to follow the neighbours. Consulting a contemporary directory for Nottingham, I found no reference to Josiah, but I did find the names of people living close by. I typed one of these into the system, found him, then moved along the street using the 'neighbours' feature. There was Josiah, after all – masquerading as 'Josiah *Ball*' ('Retired Independent Minister Graduate Edinb Univ'). All right, I know – I should have thought of that particular spelling variation at the outset! As it happens, the regional disk index refuses to recognise 'Josiah *Ball*', though the national index is happy to do so – a small glitch in the system. If Version 3 of the Resource File Viewer had been available at the time, I could have gone straight to Burns Street without the need to refer to a printed Nottingham Directory, of course.

In March 2000 Fred Wright recounted the story in *Family Tree Magazine* of a search he had made in the 1881 census for Henry Goddard, aged 80, living in Maitland Park, St Pancras. Consulting a photocopy of the original returns, Fred found Henry all right, aged 80 and still working, apparently, as a door-keeper at the House of Lords. What caught Fred's eye, however, were the neighbours: nearby was Edwin Willis, an internationally-famous organ builder, and next to him at number 41, none other than Karl Marx ('author, political economy'), his wife Jenny, their daughter Eleanor and Helen Demuth, general servant, who herself bore an illegitimate child fathered by Marx. Tom Wood, compiler of *Family Tree Magazine*'s 'Miscellany' feature, was fascinated by this story, and decided to look up Karl Marx for himself, only to find that he was no more lucky than I had been in my search for Josiah Bull: no match could be found. Tom, too, decided to beat a path to Marx's door by visiting the neighbours first, to 'creep up on it', as he put it. No, Tom and I had never discussed this strategy – it just seemed as if a lateral approach would have a lot to commend it. First finding Henry Goddard, born in 1801, Tom was duly rewarded – not with Karl Marx, but with 'Karl *Wass*'.

Susan Lumas, in *Making use of the census*, offers us two further census entries for Marx, in each of which his name is misrepresented: you'd find him in 1841 as *Charles Mark* ('doctor of Philosophy, author'), while in 1861 he was *Karl Mara* ('Philosophical author'). Marx died in 1884 and was buried in Highgate Cemetery, so he was spared the indignity of having his name distorted in any further censuses. The lesson to be learned here, however, is clear enough: the person you are seeking may have had his or her name mis-heard or mis-spelt, so if you can find out who the neighbours are, make use of them!

**Beware the nasty case of Michael Morrison

The 1871 census for 7 Charlotte Street ('The Queen's Arms'), Shrewsbury, includes the family of Michael Morrison, a 31 year old licensed victualler, born in Islington, Middlesex, together with his wife Mary from Condover, Shropshire, and their seven-month old daughter Ellen. Here, too, is Michael's lunatic mother Elizabeth, an annuitant, one general servant and a barmaid.

Not an untypical family, you may say? What makes them unusual, however, is the fact that they never existed. As a guide to enumerators who needed to know how to fill out the returns accurately, the authorities provided a specimen set of entries for a number of fictitious families as a model to follow. In 1841 we have the family of James Johnson and others; in 1851 it was the turn of Michael Mingen of Shrewsbury, who was magically metamorphosed into Michael Morrison in 1861. Michael and his family reigned supreme until 1901, when dreary old John Smith took over. Rumour has it that a number of researchers, spotting such entries at the beginning of an enumerator's book, and being hoodwinked by the fact that each entry is printed in such a way as to simulate copperplate writing, have proudly built Michael and his kin into their family trees. I don't believe a word of it, myself, though Sue Lumas tells me that she has seen a case of one enumerator who was so keen to obey instructions that he copied not only the format, but also the copperplate handwriting of the sample page when writing up his entire district.

**Expect to find bizarre, comical or wistful entries in census returns

All living creatures . . .

In the autumn of 1979, two 19th-century music-hall songs on the subject of the 1861 census were published in the journal *Local Population Studies*, and were reprinted in the October 1997 edition of the *Wiltshire Family History Society Journal*.

One of the songs contains the following verse:

> *There's one old cove named Billy Brown*
> *When the census paper was brought round,*
> *Says he "By George I must put down*
> *All my family in the census."*
> *He put down himself, his wife, then he*
> *Began to describe his family,*
> *There was Michael, Murphy, Dan and Pat,*
> *Three hens, a cock, a dog and a cat,*

Will sleep in the house on Sunday night,
If everything goes well and right,
But if the bugs and fleas so nip and bite,
They ought to be put in the census ...

There's plenty of exaggeration going on here, but also a grain of truth. An issue of the *Dunnington and Free Churchman Magazine* for 1901 was bemused to report that when the census was taken on the night of 31st March of that year, some rustic soul or other had included a domestic cat on his household return. The duly-returned moggy, name of 'Jim', was said to be a lodger, one year of age, of the male sex and single. Occupation: 'Mouse-catcher, worker on own account'. Infirmities: 'Nil'. (Gordon Higlett, *FTM*, September 1997).

Doctored entries

Dating no doubt from the days when researchers were allowed to consult the original manuscript returns, a number of witty interpolations have found their way into the records. How else would we explain the presence of 'Nell Gwynne, widow, orange seller, aged 97 ... no stated place of birth' in the 1881 return for St Andrew Undershaft in the City of London (RG11/381)? (Mrs G. Lawes, *FTM*, April 1993).

Someone also managed to doctor the 1881 return for 16 Acacia Gardens, Paddington, stating that the head of the household, Robert Goodman, was an 'International playboy' ('Handicap: Lunatic') and that his son of the same name was a 'Ponce'. A range of unlikely-sounding places of birth (Timbuctoo, Nepal, Rangpoor, Afghanistan, Syria, Lisbon, Colombo, Penal Colony, Australia ...) completed the spoof, though the hoaxer gave the game away, deliberately or accidentally, by claiming that the 31 year old footman, John Gordon, was born in Pakistan – a country, we know, which only came into existence in 1947.

In fact we can make a fair guess that this particular set of cheeky details was added at a time when researchers were allowed to consult the original returns, rather than being offered microfilm copies of them. This fictitious entry appears on page 48 of the returns, though the 'Abstract of totals' page only refers to 47 pages. Page 48, then, was originally blank, thus offering a golden opportunity for a prankster to carry out his or her nefarious business.

All deaf and dumb

You never know how many stories about the census are apocryphal, especially when the context is an Irish one, as in the following example:

1881 British Census

Dwelling: 16 Acacia Gardens
Census Place: Paddington, London, Middlesex, England
Source: FHL Film 1341004   PRO Ref RG11   Piece 0020   Folio 126   Page 48

Name	Marr	Age	Sex	Birthplace
Robert GOODMAN	**M**	**52**	**M**	**Maidstone, Kent, England**
Rel: Head Occ: International Playboy				Handicap: Lunatic
Cecily GOODMAN	M	97	F	Maidstone, Kent, England
Rel: Wife Occ: No Profession				
Robert GOODMAN	U	40	M	Maidstone, Kent, England
Rel: Son Occ: Ponce				
James GOODMAN	U	12	M	Maidstone, Kent, England
Rel: Son Occ: Scholar				
Iain SMITH	M	65	M	Timbucktoo
Rel: Servant Occ: Butler				
Nelly SMITH	M	65	F	Nepal, India
Rel: Servant Occ: Wife Dom Serv				
Alfred GREEN	U	40	M	Rangpoor
Rel: Servant Occ: Chauffur				
Abraham WILKE	U	25	M	Afghanistan
Rel: Servant Occ: Footman				
John GORDON	U	31	M	Pakistan
Rel: Servant Occ: Footman				
David KING	U	25	M	Syria
Rel: Servant Occ: Footman				
William JOHNSTONE	U	40	M	Lisbon
Rel: Servant Occ: Footman				
Mary SMART	U	20	F	India
Rel: Servant Occ: Ladys Maid				
Lizzie JONES	U	19	F	Colombo
Rel: Servant Occ: Ladys Maid				
Jean ABRANOS	U	17	F	Penal Colony, Australia
Rel: Servant Occ: Ladys Maid				
Mary WILSON	M	41	F	Timbuctoo
Rel: Servant Occ: Laundry Maid				
Elizabeth KIMMETT	U	30	F	Timbuctoo
Rel: Servant Occ: Kitchen Maid				
Mary BENNETT	U	25	F	Timbuctoo
Rel: Servant Occ: Kitchen Maid				

It's a spoof. *There was a time when researchers were allowed to consult the original census enumerators' books for England and Wales. Here is one unintended result of that liberal policy: someone has used a blank page to make a fictitious entry for 'Robert Goodman, International playboy' and his 'family'. (From the 1881 Census on CD-ROM, a joint venture by the Church of Jesus Christ of Latter-day Saints and the Federation of Family History Societies).* [Reprinted by permission. Public Record Office. Copyright © 1998, by Intellectual Reserve, Inc.]

In the census returns of 1881 it was shown that a certain district in Ireland contained an unprecedentedly large number of deaf and dumb. Not only was the record of the proportion to the hearing and speaking broken, but the relative increase in the afflicted was so alarming, that special inquiry was made into the matter, with a view to ascertaining, if possible, what were the local conditions which had brought so many afflicted mortals into existence. The explanation was at once simple and reassuring. The enumerator, with a genius for actualities thoroughly Irish, had included under the heading Deaf and Dumb all babes who had neither learnt to speak nor to understand what was said to them.

(From *The Strand Magazine*, vol.2, 1891, submitted to *FTM*, December 1998, by Ian Gray.)

Odd jobs

Even some genuinely-described jobs as stated on census returns can make us do a double-take; there are a handful of 'keel bullies' and 'tingle makers' around the place, together with a fair number of 'professional cadgers' – these being nothing more sinister than carriers, hawkers or street-sellers. More charming is the lady described as a 'Writer of Precious Promises', or Thomas Miller of Newington, 'Author of Gideon Giles, Poems, Royston Guide ...'. A nice spot of free advertising at work here! (Fred Waite, *FTM*, April 1993). An enumerator working in Limehouse, London, in 1871, described all the prostitutes he enountered as 'fallen' in the occupational column – and had a real problem, as we might imagine, in gleaning any accurate information about these good ladies' clients on census night. Some became simply 'Gentleman (Query)' or 'Jack of all trades (Nothing)' (*Making sense of the census* by Edward Higgs (1989)).

Susan Lumas has some wonderful snippets gleaned from the returns, of the sort that it would otherwise take a lifetime to unearth. She found examples of people described as: 'a professional wizard' (RG 10/4684, f.30, p.6); 'aristocratic' (with a comment added in another hand: 'Oh, dear') (HO 107/2171, f.224, p.19); a 'squatter from Queensland' (RG11/ 140, f.28,p.49); a 'nymph of the pavé' (HO 107/1508, f.578, p.36) and even one poor soul described as 'nondescript' (RG 10/1299, f.21, p.14) and another as 'generally useful' (HO 197/1528, f.229, p.11).

Sometimes, however, the head of the household seems to have welcomed the census as an opportunity to vent his or her spleen. In the 1851 census for Brampton Bierlow, near Swinton, Yorkshire, the Taylor family had Mrs Taylor's brother, Robert Johnson, lodging with them. The head of the household, William Taylor, grabbed the opportunity to make it clear what he thought of his no-good brother-in-law, and ensured that he was entered on the census as a 'spendthrift'. The enumerator, ever mindful of the need to provide meaningful statistics, had ringed this word and added: 'No occupation' (Colin Mangham, *FTM*, April 1993).

Speaking of occupations, don't assume that the term 'scholar' used of a young person was some kind of accolade, suggesting that this was a boy or girl of serious and scholarly demeanour. In 1851 a child was to be described as a 'scholar' if he or she was above five years of age and was attending school or receiving private tuition at home. Increasingly this definition was changed – and misunderstood by some enumerators, it must be said. It's hard to know what to make of the fact that Betty Thomas, writing to Jean Cole of *Family Tree Magazine* in August 2000, had found her three-times great grandmother, Elizabeth Searl, in the Norfolk census for 1851: 'Scholar, aged 49'. A few of Elizabeth's grown-up female neighbours were scholars, too – all very odd in the days before the Open University had even been dreamed of! It seems possible in this particular case that the ladies in question might have been receiving some instruction in bible reading – or in some craft skill or other – at nearby Denton House, where their husbands worked.

Odd marital condition

Occasionally, oddities creep into the column headed 'Condition as to marriage'. John Delves, a blacksmith, headed up a household at 1 Stourbridge Street, Bromsgrove, at the time of the 1891 census. There, too, was his daughter Caroline Whalley or Delves, a wrought nailmaker.

'**Condition as to marriage: Bigamist'.** *John Delves, a blacksmith living in Bromsgrove, Worcestershire, has been disarmingly frank – or mischievous – enough to list his daughter Caroline as a 'bigamist' on the 1891 census.* [PRO RG12/2344. Reproduced with permission from an original document held by the Public Record Office]

What was Caroline – unmarried, a wife, a widow? No, she is described quite unequivocally as a 'bigamist'. Later interpolation, or genuine entry? (Brenda Hughes, *FTM*, January 1994).

Odd relation to Head of Household

Certain individuals featured in the census lived in the strangest places. Susan Lumas found George Johnson of Barton-upon-Irewell 'living in an empty coke oven' (RG 9/2859, f.74, p.17), and one man was living in a shed, his relationship to the Head of Household being described simply as 'friendly' (RG 9/1783, f.35, p.22). Accurate, no doubt, but not quite the sort of answer the authorities were anticipating ...

Enumerator at his wit's end

Occasionally, tired and frustrated enumerators would let the mask slip, and add a few caustic comments of their own as they made their returns, as in this example from Marylebone in 1851:

> *All that part of the Rectory District comprising Orchard Place, Edwardes Mews and Calmel Mews, performed by Mr Spencer of 65 East Street, Manchester Square ... NB: The registrar or parties who combined the above places in union with Gray's Buildings and other streets could not have been aware of the localities, labour and difficulties of the said places, and of the impossibility of its accomplishment by one person. In Orchard Place and Gray's Buildings are about 450 rooms occupied by separate families one half of whom were unable to make out their returns on schedules, which the enumerator had to perform without a table to write on or a chair to sit upon ... Five pounds would not be a sufficient compensation for the fortnight's labour, anxiety and expense of making the returns of the two books. Thomas Panchard, No 4 Homer Place, New Road.* (Dr Ron Cox, *FTM*, August 1993)

For more information on the census you are recommended to read Susan Lumas's book, mentioned above, and for an in-depth study of the subject, see *Making sense of the census: the manuscript returns for England and Wales, 1801–1901* by Edward Higgs (HMSO [PRO] 1989), which has a particularly useful Appendix (4) in which geographical and administrative areas in the census are defined and explained.

A Final Word

I guess we can never have too much good advice. I've tried to offer some here, in a modest way, but for those of you who enjoy collections of miscellaneous genealogical material leavened with yet more hints and words of wisdom, I'd recommend that you read *The Family Tree Detective*, referred to above, and also look out for regular features in *Family Tree Magazine* such as Tom Wood's 'Genealogical Miscellany', Michael Armstrong's 'This may interest you', Cecil Humphery-Smith's 'Something to think about', Jean Cole's 'Questions and answers' and Pauline Litton's 'Pitfalls and possibilities in family history research'.

Index